I0150332

WHY BOTHER?
BECAUSE SELF-HELP
IS NEVER STUPID

TRANSFORM BEING PISSED-OFF, NUMB, in DENIAL, or EMOTIONAL INTO PEACE & PASSION

Martha Du'Sage

Copyright © 2014 by Martha Du'Sage

All rights reserved.

No part of this book may be reproduced in any form or by any
electronic or mechanical means including information storage and
retrieval systems, without permission in writing from the author.
The only exception is by a reviewer, who may quote
short excerpts in a review.

Know Time Communication Books are available through Ingram Press,
and available for order through Ingram Press Catalogues

Disclaimer: This content of this book is the direct personal
experience of the author and not to be substituted for medical
or professional help.

Visit my website at www.marthadusage.com

Printed in the United States of America

First Printing: April 2014

ISBN 978-1-62747-053-7
Ebook ISBN 978-1-62747-054-4

Dedication

To my dear friend and mentor, Janie Manning Torrens:

You didn't know me. You didn't owe me. Yet you took me under your wing and showed me that life could be different, very different.

You saw something in me that I didn't. You encouraged me. You inspired me. You showed me how to value myself.

You gave me perspective in ways that I did not see. You led me to a path that led to multiple pathways. Now, I am able to experience life and all its complexities with peace and simplicity.

I recognize, you were the first to open my eyes to the true meaning of unconditional love—something I didn't understand or have any concept of. All that I knew of love was the belief that I was unlovable.

The idea of self-love was hidden in a dusty vault deep within me, rigged to release an acid that burned through every cell of my body, especially in my throat, causing me to choke at the thought. I was taught that self-love was selfish. Selfish was something that I feared. Through your example, I can claim with sovereignty from my knowing that I am selfless.

Love is limitless inside and outside of me. This I know even when I am expressing from less than my mastery.

While you may think that I would have been okay without you; *it was you* who started the chain of events in my life that led me to embrace the full spectrum of me. It was your kindness, your honesty, your truth, experience and knowing that was a blessing.

You have been a friend, a mentor, a mother, a sister, and most of all, a guardian angel in human form to me. By being who you are, I learned much more than I could have ever expected. You possess authenticity, wisdom, and a compassion that is like a rare gem.

Though much time may pass between our visits, you are a gift that I will forever cherish and be grateful for.

Of all the people in this world who I would want to be proud of me, you would be at the top. Know that you have made an impact on not just me, but many. That's why this book is dedicated to you—my friend, my mentor, my mother, my sister, my guardian angel.

Table of Contents

Acknowledgements

My dear friend, Tracy Brooker – For all your encouragement and support. I am forever grateful.

Keith Varnum – TheDream.com - For all the mentoring in Heart-Centered, Conscious Knowing – My heart to yours.

Sabra House – The Lighthouse Center, Inc. – One sentence changed the voice of the whole book. Thank you!

Dr. David Reed – Wherever you may be. I offer my sincere gratitude.

And... to Velia for the recommendation. Thank you!

Diane Genco, MA, LPC – The Arizona Center for Change for allowing me to use your web information. Thank you!

Dr. Neil Douglas Klotz – For your work on Aramaic translations; particularly "Healing Breath" and "Blessings of the Cosmos." Thank you!

Caroline Myss – "Why People Don't Heal and How They Can." Your book changed the way I perceive. Thank you!

Neale Donald Walsh – "The Little Soul and the Sun." Thank you for helping heal my inner child.

All the Fantastic artists on my playlist – *Long Live Rock!*

Deep appreciation and gratitude to Deepak Chopra and Wayne Dyer for annoying the hell out of me; literally, helping to get "Hell" out of me.

Returned love to all the divine beings, showing up to bring this book to fruition; especially Gabriele/Gabrielle and Raphael, *I can feel you* "All Around Me" (*Flyleaf*), loving me. Thank you for showing me physical proof that needs no explanation.

My Avalon Sister, Elizabeth Costello - For never giving up on me. Much love!

Preface

Why Bother to Write this Book?

Why am I qualified? Why aren't I qualified? I come to you broken but unshackled, unburdened, and renewed. I come to you as a cracked pot. Light was allowed to shine through, and repairs made through the art of _kintsugi_. Okay, well maybe I should say heart-centered knowing, consciousness, awareness and developing intuition has changed my life from a functional dysfunctionict (yeah that's made-up), to someone who is not afraid to let her "True Colors" shine through—_Cyndi Lauper._ Give it a listen.

If you are seeking a treasured kintsugi type repair, this book may be for you. _"The world breaks everyone, then some become strong at the broken places."_ ~_Ernest Hemingway_

I moved away from my roots to heal and have risen from the ashes, not realizing how metaphoric moving to Phoenix would be. Cliché? Maybe? Sometimes we are more broken then we know, but with a little effort, we discover we aren't broken at all.

One thing for certain that I have observed in all my self-help, heart-centered experiences is that we all have similar issues. Different players, different story lines, different levels, varying degrees, unique twists, but it all equates to similar drama. I was conditioned to live in denial to the point of creating suppressed memory. I was a master at letting my wounded ego take over in its failed attempt to protect me and discovered protection wasn't even needed. Do I still get my buttons pushed? Oh yeah, but not nearly as often. My mastery has crossed a point of convergence on the spectrum of life. Now, I choose, when and how I participate, if at all. Does it always appear gracious?

No. Why? The fact is, the truth of some topics is uncomfortable for others even when we make a conscious effort to express honestly. Expressing truth from you heart is not unkind, it's honest.

Will I change my views? Will I wish I said more? Will I wish I said less? Will I wish I said things differently? Seriously? Yuk! That's exactly the kind of thought process, self-speak, idle chatter, and self-doubt that I want to help you avoid, one of the *why bother*s of this book. The more we open and expand, the more our viewpoints change, the more our world fills with light and color. I will trust that you will get whatever you need out of this book. I trust your needs will change, and I trust that you can change the outcome of your story.

I was guided to write this book, because there were so many things I misinterpreted along the path. I've had quite a few "aha" moments, and I AM in an "I AM" space that is much deeper than just a level of maturity you get with age. If you are reading this, you must have some level of interest in transforming your life to a deeper level of consciousness, and you can, no matter how blessed or messed-up your story appears.

We all misperceive at some point, but once some of the common misinterpretations are understood, we perceive with not only a broadened perspective, but an expanded one, opening up a world of possibilities and betterment. Maybe the only thing you will discover is that we all have shared experiences. If so, then this book might help you find humor or validation in knowing you are not alone. We are never alone. It only feels that way sometimes, and your experiences should never be trivialized. In the divine connectedness to the cosmos, when you are ready, there is always someone or something there to pick you up.

When I say divine, interpret that as you wish. Atheist or believer, define divine as you choose or don't define it at all. Regardless of your perception, all of us are connected to this planet and to the cosmos. If we allow it, consciousness shows us truth. Whether you believe the soul continues or not, there is much to be gained from seeking peace and living in integrity.

Listening to so many others say "I just don't get it," drove me to say, "I can help if you want." That's why I bothered.

This life is your path, and you can navigate it your way. Regardless of what you contracted to do before you manifested as human, your free will offers you the opportunity to choose. Choosing consciousness helps us choose more wisely. If you find you haven't chosen wisely, then find a way to grow from it. Choose gratitude and embrace the lessons so you can choose more wisely next time. We are all on the path to remembering who we are and why we are here, and we awaken when our time is ripe. Thank you, *Dr. Neil Douglas-Klotz* for providing us with a perspective of something being "ripe," rather than right or wrong, through your Aramaic translations of the words of, the one we call, "Jesus," which provide us with a way to express without judgment. Less judgment is sorely needed.

Regardless of the path you choose, I wish good morning to your divine awakening, as I simply wish that you find much joy along the way filled with lots of clarity and *aha* moments. That reminds me of a song that will make your heart soar: "Mornin'" by *Al Jarreau*. In reaching you may discover the importance of your own "why bothers."

Throughout the book, there will be lots of song suggestions. As the song suggestions are made, I invite you to take a break, listen and read the lyrics which can be found at www.marthadusage.com. Synchronicity creates a desirable connection. Music helps us tap into our heart and is intended for the listener to make their own interpretation. If you don't like my suggestions, allow the music in your heart to be heard. Explore what makes your heart soar, just like Al Jarreau's song suggests. Listen to the song, read the lyrics anytime you feel the need to reach out your hand.

"That's one of the greatest things about music. You can sing a song to 85,000 people and they'll sing it back for 85,000 different reasons."—Dave Grohl

Introduction

The Twenty Questions of "Why Bother"

So, really, why bother with another self-help book? To figure that out, let's start by playing the twenty questions of "Why Bother?" Like the twenty questions, you may be familiar with, there is no lying allowed.

"Why bother"; even with the myriad of books and information available to us about self-help, healing, transformation, consciousness, awakening, enlightenment—whatever you want to call it—so many are feeling frustrated, confused, restless, overwhelmed, and just plain angry. Is this you? Have you tried self-help, knowing that it has benefits but ended up feeling disappointed? Are you wondering why others seem to be making changes yet feeling like you aren't? Are you left wondering why it worked for a while but not entirely? The thing is there isn't just one easy fix. There may be things lying below the surface that you may not have discovered yet let alone dealt with. Often it is the unseen, the unconscious, and the unembraced parts of the self that are blocking our progress no matter what fixes we have tried. There may be possibilities and perspectives that haven't yet been considered or entered your awareness. Sometimes we just don't know what we don't know until we know it. If there is an intuitive knowing that you just can't shake or a disturbance in your force, that's a good why bother.

So, really, why bother? Believe it or not, when we incarnate, we come here to learn to remember who we are. Since we all came here to remember, it makes sense that on many levels, we are all striving for the same things: *peace, freedom, fulfillment, love,* and *joy.* And guess what, we all deserve that. Have you found yourself longing for these things?

Stop for a second and say each of those words to yourself with a deep breath, holding each of them for a moment. Then give it a nice complete exhale.

Peace

Freedom

Fulfillment

Love

Joy

How did that make you feel? Good, right?

Sadly, much stress, frustration, anger, hatred, pain, and judgment resides in our world and it exists to a degree that is much greater than necessary for us to feel and comprehend the opposite more positive feelings. Most stressors come from some form of abuse. To really break free and break the dysfunctional cycles we have been in, we must continue to strive for more positive aspects and find ways to ultimately reach peace. The truth is we all crave these things, beyond just lip service or going through the motion. We want to know what these aspects feel like on the inside without pretending.

Ultimately, we want to *really feel* a sense a peace, no matter which direction the pendulum is swinging over the spectrum of life.

Often, to achieve peace, we must begin at a level of acceptance. Acceptance is felt lower in the body and more deeply rooted. So, now, let's pause and try breathing that word:

Acceptance

As you breathe that in, you may notice it in a different area of your body. For now, just quietly notice anything you notice about the feeling of acceptance.

Are you beginning to understand the idea of "why bother"? While the possibility of combining the world of divine spirit with the world of the physical absolutely exists, the number one problem that I see today in attempting to connect our contemplative life with everyday life is that we are still over intellectualizing spirituality. Consciousness is made tangible by practicing, so that it becomes integrated into our being, and in turn, into everyday life and our present-moment experiences. It's not as difficult as it may sound. Is our intellect involved? Absolutely! Much of what we have tried requires a deeper understanding and to be anchored into the knowing that comes from our heart. Everything we know is continually evolving and there is always something new to learn. We could start by learning a deeper appreciation of why we are here and what we signed up for. Appreciation creates a sense of peace, as do all the other words. As we learn to appreciate, we can learn to appreciate ourselves, who we are, why we are here, and everything around us.

Appreciation

Now, we have added to our list of things we all want. Breathe that in once for yourself. Breathe it a second time for everything and everyone around you. Breathe it in, really deep, a third time for a moment of peace. Ah!

You may sense or notice that these words we just worked with seem to start at the top of our heads and work their way down. This is the beginning of creating a divine direct connection to pure source and being firmly grounded at the same time. As you learn to appreciate and embrace the full spectrum of who you are, gratitude appears naturally.

Again, why bother? Because there are so many promises of instant fixes in this world, and we fall prey to them. While the instant fix is possible, we are often left feeling unsatisfied after getting what we *thought* we wanted. We have been searching outside of ourselves when our solutions come from within. The outside world provides clues. It's the inner world that provides solutions.

Would you like to find a way to unlock that which is within? As creatures of habit, we resist change. Have you considered what it would feel like if you allowed yourself to embrace change? Are you ready, willing and able to embrace the full spectrum of you?

Just give it a try. Close your eyes, take a breath, and imagine giving yourself an embrace. If you like, take it a step further and actually give yourself an embrace. Notice how this slows your over-thinking. Notice how your awareness becomes more centered and present.

Why bother? Because we all struggle and suffer in some way, and we want it to end. Life comes with challenges. Sometimes we just don't know what we just don't know. We might think we know, but it turns out, we don't. We are all seekers of something. Mostly, we seek answers and solutions. It's our job to find out for ourselves how we can do that from a place of peace. It's our job to learn how to express from a place of truth where we can feel at peace in our entire being, no matter what the outcome of any situation may be. Ask yourself, *how could or would it feel to make choices that no matter the outcome, I could/would be at peace?* Interchange the words to sense possibilities.

We like absolutes, and spirituality is often presented as an abstract. We like knowns, and consciousness presents us with unknowns. Often, the unknowns and lessons are presented to us in metaphor. There was a point when I said to my spiritual guides, "Okay, everybody, I am grateful for the clues, but I need you to break it down in terms that I can understand. After having a tangible experience, then I can go back to the metaphor and say, 'oh yeah, now I get it'. Often, it is the process of tick-tocking back and forth that allows us to see the message more clearly because we are observing from a broader perspective.

Would you like your internal guidance to become easier for you to recognize, see, hear, notice, feel, and utilize with clarity and confidence? Ideally, it serves us to develop all aspects of awareness.

We all think we want stability: financial stability, family stability, stability in relationships, stability in our jobs, and stability in our economy. We fail to recognize that we are living on rock that is continuously moving through space, spinning at some great speed, with molten lava under our feet. So what is stability, really? How do we create that for ourselves in this tumultuous world? And how would it feel if we did?

The Buddhists say *everything is in a constant state of decay.* Everything we experience is in a constant state of flux. Your stability lies in your ability to create and maintain a connection between the divine and being grounded simultaneously in the earth body you were given. Two points converge to make one. You are that point. But consider expanding beyond the straight and narrow. The straight and narrow path isn't always as righteous as we have been led to believe.

More often than not, the narrow perspective is exactly what creates conflict, need, frustration, hatred, judgment, and discontent, which adds up to compounded fear. Fear plus abuse, is a basis of all problems that have existed since the dawn of third-dimensional time. Abuse is something that is too often swept under the rug because people find it uncomfortable to discuss. The word hate either carries too much conviction or is too often trivialized.

At this point in the evolution of humanity, it is essential to learn how to **expand** our consciousness. Expanding our consciousness leads to integrating all aspects of who we are. Integration leads to integrity, and the only true stability is the stability we create through integrity.

We can also equate the molten lava under our feet to what happens when we don't deal with lies below the surface of our consciousness. Something is brewing in our subconscious. Eventually, all that boiling lava wants somewhere to go. How it erupts, how it impacts us, and how it impacts those around us requires consideration. How would it feel if you could respond more ideally in most situations and take responsibility for your actions when you don't? Take that a step further and consider how it would feel to learn how to forgive yourself and others for being human.

Why bother? Because: we all have something to forgive or be forgiven for. Too often, we are quick to place blame, forgetting our role in the story, forgetting our own personal responsibility in the equation. This is not about wallowing in regret either direction. Accountability, yes, blame, no. It's about stepping into integrity where we can find a place of pure acceptance.

Let's try this again. Acceptance: Breathe that word into your consciousness. Acceptance. Observe how that feels.

Now, try it again with "appreciation." This time try pulling the word "appreciation" from the bottom of your feet up into the root chakra at the base of your spine. Take a second breath and pull the idea of appreciation into your heart center. Breathe the word a third time from the heart up over your head and let the feeling fill you and surround you.

We can use our internal volcanic eruptions for so many better things. After all, it is that molten lava that has created the earth under our feet upon which we walk and has created a sense of stability in an unstable world. We can begin to view the eruption as Mother Earth's transformative power that provides us with stability and support as a means to heal beyond just coping. We can use it to fuel passion.

Why bother? Because we need to be encouraged to practice heart-centered consciousness, so it becomes the prevailing zeitgeist, which leads us to a life filled with gusto, enthusiasm, and purpose.

As cliché as this may sound, humor me. Not expanding consciousness is like keeping ourselves stuck in the belief that the earth is the center of the universe. Have you ever considered how metaphoric that belief still is? The earth being the center represents our ego and our belief that everything revolves around us. After allowing yourself to experience the words we breathed into being, how does being the center of the universe make you feel? Not as good, huh? Why? Because it makes us feel alone and separate. Now that we have a sense of how we can feel differently, we can take that intellectually known metaphor and begin to transform it into a heart-centered knowing.

Many have achieved and/or made progress towards heart-centered consciousness. Sadly, much of the same type of arrogance attached to old beliefs still exists today. This is why it's up to us. It's not possible for anyone else to initiate change, because there is only "us."

We must choose between the red pill and the blue pill. Look at the metaphor and look at your life. You decide.

Third inspirational song suggestion: "You Decide" by *Fireflight*. Listen and decide for yourself if "love can change your life."

Would you agree that knowing that there is only "us" is a really good reason to make heart-centered consciousness fully integrated into our being? Does this idea resonate enough for you to put your ego into a time-out?

Why bother? Because there are still too many who believe they are not worthy of enlightenment. Those who are starting to awaken often *think* enlightenment is only for the gurus, monks, lamas, shamans, and priests. This simply is not true. Enlightenment *IS* for *ALL* of us. We came here to master third dimension and find our way back to the light. **<u>You</u>** can take the journey inward and live a contemplative life. *It can be a part of everyday living.* Ask yourself: What options have I rejected needlessly? Which of these options can I accept now?

Why bother? Because: we live in a world of contradiction—which creates confusion—leading to the self-defeating belief of I-don't-know-what-to-do. Heart-centered consciousness teaches us what we do know and shows us the right thing to do for ourselves without judgment or doubt. Practicing will allow you/us/them/me to expand into whatever is beyond the things that are no longer okay or acceptable. It is time for all of us to practice. If not now, when? Being heart-centered doesn't make you a wimp. It makes you strong, vibrant, and powerful. Can this planet afford to continue on the self-destructive trajectory it is on? Are you denying personal power into your life by saying, "I don't know"? Have you considered what fears might be holding you back? Have you considered that saying, "I don't know" is simply fear? Are you ready to harness your power and do your part to take the planet back for all of us and not just the few who have selfishly put themselves in a place of power?

How about putting power on your list? Power. Breathe it in—power—pure divine power without control, constraints, or restrictions, just power of the divine.

If someone thinks that consciousness is weird, here is my take on this:

Tell them that the definition of "weird" is supernatural, and you prefer supernatural over mundane any day.

Again, why bother? Because: we live in so much judgment around us: judgment of self, judgment of others, judgment of ideas, fear of being judged, and judgment of judging, which leaves us with a lot of injustice. Instead, how would it feel to join a justice league?

Let's add to the *Supernatural* mix. Does anyone think Sam and Dean are wimps? Maybe they should be added to the list of superheroes. Do you judge the show as too violent for your spirituality to allow you to watch it? Do you judge it because there are demons in the show? We live in a violent world, and we all have demons to fight until we reach peace. We have to face the demons. How do you defeat an enemy you don't know? If you look below the surface, it would appear, there are some things that are more real than we are willing to admit. The story is a metaphor for living in integrity—a classic example of struggle between good and evil that resides in all of us. No matter how humanly flawed, they try to do the right thing, and the brothers *support* each other. And...oh, so handsome! Sorry, slight distraction. Whew!

To move beyond and step into whatever our role is, we first "have to" *feel* on a practical level. It's difficult to understand what any particular feeling is unless you have experienced it. If you don't have an understanding of a feeling, you can step back to imagine. If we can't imagine, we can take another step back to ponder—which opens the possibility to imagination. But to lead to feeling, we must radiate the imagination from the heart. If you can't imagine from the heart, go ahead and ponder from the head to the heart, sending the feeling back and forth until you get there. Let pondering, imagination, and feeling bounce around in your physical being. Everything spiritual and emotional is contained within our physical being. That's the mind-body-spirit connection that has become mainstream but is still being over intellectualized.

Simply by saying "have to," which is limiting, tells me that there is something even beyond what we already know in the area of heart-centered consciousness and present-moment awareness. We won't know what that is until we master third dimension, master life.

Why bother? Because: how often do you hear someone say they feel "stuck"? How often do you feel stuck? Imagine your feet stuck deep in mud, shit, or cement and can't get out. It doesn't feel so good, does it? It's just energy. Being stuck is another false perception that can be changed. It's a form of fear. If we really want lasting change, we need to take responsibility for getting ourselves out of whatever the muck we are in. Doing so begins in our senses.

When someone told me years ago that I wasn't in touch with my feeling, I was seriously pissed. Yeah, that joke was on me. Divinity definitely has a sense of humor. At that time, I may or may not have defended myself by bringing up things that worked some, but not enough, or I may have emotionally shut down. The old crap always found a way to not only resurface but sometimes erupt. Was it that I just had more to master? Ya think? Every thought space in my ego mind would have attempted to justify my ego-based emotions. After all, I had gone to workshops, I had gone to counseling, and I was reading books on self-help and spirituality, along with receiving energy work. I "thought" my ego was in check. The reality was that I had not fully integrated with the heart center, because I hadn't broken down the fortress around my heart, plus I didn't know my ego as well as I thought I did. Why? Because I simply didn't know enough about *the* ego, let alone *my* ego. Anger would have shaken me and left me wondering "how dare they say that to me." Not feel it? How ridiculous? Of course I feel it. I'm angry, aren't I? That's feeling, isn't it? When you have suffered abuse, one word can throw you into the past trauma. Now, I not only comprehend the difference between feeling and emotion, but I can appreciate that the intensity of the anger shaking inside my body was exactly the disturbance I needed to let my passion erupt and persevere in learning to embrace the ego for what the human experience is.

Sometimes what we don't want is exactly what we need. So before anyone gives up and says, "I want to feel less, not more," the feeling I am talking about is not the same as over-emotional sensitivity or under-emotional numbness, or the in-between of denial. Denial has its own spectrometer. That's where all the excuses come in. Most of us simply have not been taught about heart-centered feeling and emotional feeling which is why we don't know how to cope with our emotions or ego. Rather than learn to live consciously, we go into denial or numbness. If you need pills to get over a rough spot, that's okay. However, if you become dependent and only listen to what others say, instead of what your intuitive or integrated self says, you may retard your journey. Exercise caution and discernment. We can only discover our true feelings through self-exploration. In that self-exploration, you may find yourself playing at opposite ends of the spectrum of emotion, until you reach a place that feels like stability. It's okay. Ride it until you find a place where you say to yourself, *Oh, I like it here; this feels like home.*

Feeling begins the process of ***integration.*** Once you feel and learn to stay in the heart center, integration is inevitable. From there, we can learn to ***expand*** "it."

What does that mean?

I am referring to feeling from the heart center, integration of our being, and expansion of our consciousness. There is more to the expansion of our consciousness than just coming from our heart. We are beginning to understand the difference between left-brain and right-brain thinking, but it is important not to wrong one side or the other. It is important not to wrong any part of the process while we learn to become integrated, and that includes thinking. This way there is no neglect of self on any level, and we can learn to be self-nurturing.

Emotion from the ego and self-judgment can be where miscreation begins. Heart-based feeling allows for creation from our passion. Without integration of the entire self, we run the risk of having joy taken away (self-sabotage) after creating something wonderful because there is more to be revealed and/or something in our being is requiring attention, nurturing or some form of assistance. That doesn't make you wrong; it's just part of the journey.

This is why to become whole and fulfilled, it is in all our best interest to dig below the surface and make sure all parts of self are cared for. If not, there can be a breakdown or disconnect, which creates a miscreation. That's logical, right?

In the beginning, I intellectualized consciousness, too. At times I still do. I had no choice. I didn't know what feeling felt like, but I made the choice to try. I had to ponder, imagine and intellectualize feeling until I got to know it. Now there are times, I feel it and then I intellectualize it. In third dimension, where we currently live, it is all about opposites, duality, and contradiction. At times, recognizing this and working through it can be quite maddening, as it leaves us feeling frustrated, judging ourselves, believing we are right or wrong, questioning and doubting. With practice, you'll get there. Or maybe we should take the Bob Newhart approach: "Stop it." Stop beating yourself up and cooperate with yourself.

This is why practice is so important. Really, isn't practice important to all aspects of learning? Even the word "practical" contains the word "practice." So, if you want to awaken and become enlightened, why wouldn't you practice? Enlightenment— it's not all esoteric foo-foo and does not require you to run around in white robes.

Why bother? Because the age-old questions of -*Why are we here?*—*What am I supposed to do? What is my purpose?*—still exist. We all want answers that will lead to fulfillment on a deeper level than our boxes from the Amazon Fulfillment Center, even though they bring excitement and joy when they are delivered. We all came here to master third dimension, master life. How about starting by being the master of one—you. That doesn't mean you stomp on other people like a slave master. Master yourself using the quality of equality and integrity. Saying that we don't care is just quitting. We never know what we are capable of until we try. Even if you experience pain, perseverance will pay off.

Why bother? Because we are still going through life blindfolded, and then we feel blindsided. How many things in your life have you blindly accepted? How many things should you no longer accept? What things are just not okay? Which things can you accept or learn to accept? What will create peace inside of you? What would create harmony? How about creating insight, intuition, and intimacy with yourself and your world? Your intuition will guide you, blindfolded or not. Are you willing to allow your intuition and your will to take over and make lasting changes?

Why bother? Wouldn't it feel really great if you knew exactly what your soul desired, what your true purpose was, and if you could do that with peace in your heart? Aren't you tired of the same old, same old when the same old doesn't work anymore? What is the alternative? Never knowing? Be brave, be strong, be courageous, and make the choice of knowing.

Why bother? Because often there are concepts that you have to hear over and over again until you finally start to listen. Often you need to hear a message multiple times and/or from multiple sources until it "sinks in," until it integrates, incorporates, and cooperates.

Once we have integrated all parts of ourselves, our integrity is not tested so often.

Ready for some intentional redundancy?

Why bother? Because you have to hear it over and over until you finally start to take charge of your life. Hear it until you move beyond the intellect. Start to practice and do whatever it takes to make lasting changes that will help to raise your vibration and the vibration of the whole planet. We have to keep trying to make this world a better place to live for everyone. You are part of the whole. Participate or disintegrate! As Yoda said, "Do or do not. There is no try."

Many of us have heard stories of transformation that while having a resonance of truth, seem too fantastical. We have resistance or blocks to believing we can create transformation for ourselves, and we allow others' doubts to stop us when we fear rejection. If you are being attracted to the intoxicating scent of transformation, follow it with the gentleness of a bloodhound. The trail may lead you to a "magical mystery tour" (by, *The Beatles*) that takes you away to a place where you may find acceptance of who you really are.

It helps to tap into all our senses, including the sixth sense, so that we can step into what could be our seventh sense, which is consciousness. Be aware that a sixth sense of psychic ability doesn't automatically mean the seventh sense has been fully developed. Remember Jesus' words, "All this I do, you shall do and more." Let's honor his teaching rather than keeping ourselves small.

Why bother? Because: we are often victims of the sound bite. We often misinterpret much of what we hear or what we are being taught and our ego gets angry simply because we don't understand. Consciousness provides the clarity to let go of the anger, the judgment, resentment, and whatever other uncomfortable feelings you are experiencing. What makes you angry? When you catch yourself getting angry, will you allow yourself to reflect on that anger and discover what is in the reflection?

To say it's impossible to cover everything in one book is an understatement. This journey is a journey of a lifetime, and most likely infinitely more than just that. This book's intention is to offer a few pointers to create a quickening of understanding your journey. We all come with our own unique story line. The idea is not to beleaguer my story; instead, maybe something in the story will spark an understanding within your own remembering of who you really are and that we all came here to have unique experiences while we gain mastery. I want to inspire you to be courageous in breaking down the barriers that have held you back from creating your own divine direct connection to pure source, and your own divine spark of wisdom.

This book may not mention one thing that you haven't already heard. Perhaps, in hearing something one more time, an "aha" will be created. Suddenly, coincidences will begin to occur, or are they synchronicities? Are they messages to help you remember? Is it tapping into collective memory? The important thing is that you are tapping into your awareness.

Hopefully, the next generation will have more collective memory on the idea of consciousness and peace than they do on war and conflict. It may sound idealistic, but how will we get there without practicing ways that bring more peace? Peace begins inside of each of us.

Why bother? Because it's time to recognize that it's not all about *me*; it's not all about *you*. It's not all about *us* and *them*. Cool, turned out to be a *Pink Floyd* reference ("Us and Them," good song choice for discussing us, them, who is who, and conflict). This is about all of us. All of us are the _who_ of the story. Why do you think Dr. Seuss called it "Whoville"? Recognize that there are two sides to everything. That's the **what**. You may want to explore your story for the difference in when it is about you and when it is about them by getting to know yourself. That is the _when_. Learn to put responsibility where responsibility belongs. Get your shit together and learn to put shit where shit belongs. That's the _why_. If you want to add _where_, right here right now, in present moment. It's your choice whether or not to change the whos, whats, whens, whys, and wheres of your story.

Since this book is for you and not about me, I would suggest a pause and ask yourself, "What parts of my life are in conflict? What conflicts do I really want to let go of?"

I used to wonder why I had so much conflict in my life and what lesson was I missing. Why did I have to keep facing it? Finally, after asking numerous times, the mirror finally showed me that I was a creator, but the picture was bigger and more purposeful. Sometimes it's not just about us, but also about what we allow. When I shifted my focus, I could see that I was expecting others to be in the same emotional space that I was in. Seeing this helped me let go of, to say the least, a lot.

As you read on, you will read more about "it's not all about you" and "two sides to every story." Conflict always has more than one side. In an attempt to resolve conflict, it is a good idea to sideline limiting perspectives while treading lightly in another's shoes. Please, only do that as an observer, teacher, or problem solver, not as a controller or fixer. Even with the sincerest intent, if our ego is not in check, the conflict may not be resolved.

While you are observing, you may learn to discern, so you can use common sense in deciding what is true or not true, what is fact and what is fiction, what is illusion and what is real, what you chose to believe and not to believe, what has value and what does not, and what to keep and what to toss away. Learning to discern is critical when you are creating your own reality. Learning discernment will help you to develop trust in your intuition and in turn yourself. As the *Pink Floyd* song says, "Who knows which is which and who is who." As you learn discernment, you may feel yourself naturally becoming more grounded and notice when you are not. This will help you learn to know when it's time to ask for help.

So, why bother? Because: change requires effort to become effortless. How profound do you want your changes to be? What are you willing to do to implement lasting change and anchor it into your being? What would it feel like if your life became a rhythmic dance that flowed effortlessly even throughout the challenges we face, encouraging you to take a leap of faith?

As many of us believe there are no accidents, calling anything a mistake also feels very limiting. We can all be divinely connected while being grounded at the same time. This is living in the present moment. Living in the present moment truly is a choice. It's for you to decide if you want to wake up or stay asleep. It may seem like work, the world you think you know most likely will crumble, but the payoff is immeasurable. Give yourself a little responsibility and accountability check and ask yourself, "Am I willing to allow some parts of my life to crumble away knowing that there is something better waiting?" If the answer is yes, then ask, "Am I willing to put out the effort for my life to become effortless?" "Let the sleeper awaken" (Reference to *Dune* by Frank Herbert). Are you ready to awaken and see that lasting transformation is possible?

"Yes. Okay, okay…we, your readers, get it now. Please stop, please stop."

Fine, just let me finish the last of the twenty questions. That was a lot of "why bothers."

Why bother? When you take charge and take personal responsibility for your life, you will learn to communicate more clearly, concisely and express more freely, and, with that, you will learn a new meaning of cooperation. The universe will have no choice but to allow joy into your life. Isn't that what we all want, more joy?

Let's take a joy breath. Ready, breathe in JOY! Hold it, hold it, feel it. Now let it out. JOY!

Sometimes I can't help but continue trying to make a point even when I am cognizant of the danger of appearing like it is idle chatter. Sometimes I use the "wah wa wah" on my guy just to see if he is still listening. Does anyone else do that or have it done to them? It's not about being right, which the repetition may appear to be. There are "just so many"—limited or "just so many"—expanded ways to express. I happen to get excited by options, colors and possibility.

There is much complexity to life, emotion, and feeling—much that we create unnecessarily; much that is there to create wonder. One of our challenges is learning to turn seeming complexities into simplicities, or take something simple and make it intricate. It works both ways. Often we find answers in breaking down the complexity into its smaller components. The opposite also exists when we look at the fine details and then step back and look at the big picture: two sides to every story and the multiple facets in between and around, until we find the place we chose to reside and call it home, with complete comfort being in our own skin.

In the past, or should I say, at another point in my life, I wasn't sure if my ability to see both sides of a story was a blessing or a curse. I know the answer now—blessing, definitely a blessing.

And...to offer an excuse for beleaguering all the "why bothers"— an excuse, Martha, really, how third-dimensional!—I guess one of my blessings and curses is that one of my animal totems is from the badger family, more specifically, a wolverine. Sometimes I have a hard time not badgering or being perceived as one who badgers. Did I say guess? What I know is that I have learned to integrate the wolverine, so it cooperates. It remains docile, as is its nature, until it is messed with; such a misunderstood creature. Let's leave it at that.

Let's listen to *Paramore's* "We Are Broken," but then ask yourself, "What must we do to be restored?"

Chapter 1

Taking the Journey

In the past I undervalued myself and what I could offer. I assumed (*and we know what that means*) that if I knew something, then so did everyone else and probably more.

I used to say that I was a student of consciousness. Suddenly, I found myself being asked for advice on a regular basis. I'd hear; "You always seem so calm, how do you do that" or I'd hear someone say, "You should ask Martha." The moment of recognition and validation as to just how far I had come, happened when a friend back east told me she made a bracelet with beads that said "WWMD" (what would Martha do). That moment came with a great deal of humility as I was reminded of all the things we shared, all the good things I left behind to achieve freedom, and a prayer that I had said for years which was *to walk a Christed path.*

After much practice, the time must come when the student lets go of doubt to be the master even if the master still has challenges and a lot more to learn. For knowledge and wisdom to have value, it must be shared. I have asked, searched, explored, and practiced. I have taken breaks; threatened the divine that I was going back to sleep; changed direction; found myself going in circles, taken steps backwards; and fallen on my ass. According to some, I possess a great deal of resilience. That must be true, because I always end up getting back on the horse, getting back on the path, and having my eyes a bit more open, ready for the next transformative adventure even if at some point I felt suicidal.

Some things I have held on to, and other things, I've let go. The breaks, the changes of direction had great value. It's the idea of holding on to what serves. Occasionally stepping off the path towards enlightenment provides the clarity required to put you back on the path. Allowing moments of joy in between keep us going.

You could say that my training is intentionally unconventional. The rebellious nature of the unconventional has helped me to break down the concept of labels and limiting beliefs. While I accept that some conventions have value, I appreciate how the unconventional expands what is possible.

When I first started my journey, I heard so many say, after just one workshop, "I want to be a facilitator, a healer, a light worker." I understood wanting to always be in this *new-to-us* energy we were learning about since every workshop was a life-transforming experience, but I was still skeptical of the depth to which it could be made real.

Recognizing that we often have to feel pain before we are *willing* to let our *will* take over to initiate change, I was seeing many come out of high-end *power of the positive* workshops on a rah-rah high, but it wore off seemingly just as quickly. Often they were left feeling like they were back to square one, or they sounded like people from certain types of MLMs that trap you in an elevator with that crazed-glazed look in their eyes, telling you that you can get rich selling absolutely nothing, almost as if an addiction has been created.

Not all, but some were being lured to workshops by the idea that they could manifest more money; seeing money as the solution to all problems. But, more often than not, if money is the first thing that we attempt to heal in our lives, we end up disappointed. Money is support, so is support what some are really seeking? Money can create a false sense of support and power with an attitude of "I'll show them" even in the most well-intended individual. How many times have you heard that the best revenge against an ex is to get rich? You've heard that, right? But is that healthy? Everyone is different, so I really am not judging or criticizing anyone's desire to be more successful. Money makes our outside world more enjoyable. Going for the gold may have worked for some, but that way would not have worked for me. I had much more lying below the surface that required healing.

Making money lured me too, but more than that, I wanted to KNOW that change could be carried into the everyday world without the quest for false power through the ego. I knew this was possible, and I felt small permanent changes. But what would it take to fully resonate with change? I had to ponder before I could feel. I had to use imagination to ponder how to feel. Imagining is not all in our imagination, as many of us have been taught. It begins the creative process and the creation of a more fulfilled life.

I wanted reassurance that change would be made in me, no matter who or what I was dealing with. I wanted to apply what I learned to everyday crap. I wanted to see that we could indeed blend the world of business, which is filled with unconscious beliefs, and the world of being awake and conscious. Especially since, in the past, the two worlds were viewed as separate and often still are, brought about by greed even by those who deny that greed exists within them. Since greed exists in our world, it does exist in all of us, just to varying degrees, and tips to the other end of the spectrum, which is generosity. There is another key word here; did you notice it? It's separate. So much could be said about separation but for now let's just say that greed is a product of the perception that we are separate.

I wanted to see if I could plant seeds even if tiny. I wanted to see if I could put a chink in the armor of people around me who were completely unconscious, no matter if I was recognized for the effort or not. This would be a challenge as I was quite broken. At the time, still in deep in denial, I didn't know just how broken I was. The mask I wore was so elaborate that I portrayed myself as not wearing one at all even to me. A spark of knowing drove me to explore. My will was that spark. It was not willfulness. It was my free will to choose freedom.

I wanted to learn to "incorporate" consciousness into my daily behavior. That incorporation has been transformed to integration. Integration leads to a deeper level of integrity. Even the words hint to us to go "in". Denial is dishonest. Deep down, no matter what, I wanted truth. I wanted honesty and I was willing to work through any pain that truth and honesty created. They say what doesn't kill us makes us stronger. Truth can be so painful that it makes us feel like we want to die, but truth can't really kill us, and the pain begins to subside when we find appreciation and acceptance.

Over and over again, we still hear how someone has written affirmations, made a vision board, asked for guidance, bought a Chinese money frog, spun around three times and thrown salt over their shoulder, watched a popular movie on manifesting dreams, been to workshop after workshop, and yet they still are not satisfied. Why? We are still looking for an outside fix when what is needed is an inside fix. When things lie below the surface unhealed, we miscreate self-sabotage unconsciously.

We have an inner and outer world, so we must give attention to both if we are to have balance. The things we use outside ourselves are tools to keep us focused, to keep us grounded and lead us to discovery. They are totems. They are not the solution. Now this might cause some raised eyebrows, but religion is a tool, too. The tool won't fix you. You have to implement the tool. Why bother buying a tool if you aren't going to implement it? Unfortunately, holding onto a particular tool at times also creates a limiting belief that it's the best or only tool, and when we aren't making progress, we blame the tool rather than search for and try another one.

Sometimes, when we try different tools, we feel like nothing works, or we have failed, and that is simply not true. Allow yourself to notice the value and open up to other possibilities. Why bother to seek if you already believe something isn't going to work? Perhaps it's a lesson in the discernment of believing or intuition. We are ALL seekers of something; otherwise, we wouldn't be feeling a restlessness that drives us to seek.

Getting attached to one tool is like an addiction, and addiction is a form of abuse. Intellectually, we all know that addiction and abuse are not healthy. Being stuck in our intellect and solely focused on logic, is illogical, defies nature, and is not integrated with our heart center where we can break free of the belief that we are unworthy of being divine beings of light. We are all worthy. If we are too attached to one thing, we tend to focus on the problem and not the possibilities that lead to a solution. When you find a tool that works, use it to its capacity, but allow yourself to recognize when it's time to move beyond and into the great beyond.

Where do you want your attention? Energy goes where attention flows. Most likely, you have heard this. So where is it? Do you need a reminder to pay attention? When a challenge presents itself, practice being the observer and then step back into a tangible actualized experience. Step into the observer again, allow the intellect to comprehend how it worked or didn't, and let your heart answer. Then, step back into the participant; allow nature to take over and participate differently. Participate or disintegrate. Become conscious or come back and do it all over again. Disintegrate doesn't have to be total decay. It can simply mean not integrated. You could use dis-integration as a tool to let go of old ways that no longer serve a purpose. Make the choice karma or no karma? Are you ready to "Break the Cycle" (*Staind*).

We all have the same basic programming, hard wiring, and dreams. We all have the same basic problems. So maybe we need to stop judging problems as we seek solutions. That doesn't mean we should make excuses for our problems, which only invites in more drama. While each of our stories has unique twists, the premise and underlying themes remain. Having the same underlying challenges is further evidence that we are all here to master third dimension, to master the human experience and support each other.

When a problem presents itself, rather than beat yourself for being unable to find appreciation and gratitude—if you recognize the judgment you have placed upon yourself for having the problem—it

5

may be easier to let go, because you now have considered both sides of the spectrum and recognize the place in the middle that brings comfort.

I should have come to this conclusion years ago when I had a divine visit. Should have? Really? Did I just say "should"? Oui or Oy? I was awakened by bright lights flashing in my eyes. As I opened them, the bright light continued, and at some point I do recall seeing 3:33. A bit disoriented, I momentarily questioned my sanity. Typically, an experience like this would have raised fear. This time there was none. I knew...I knew who this was. He said, "Martha, release your self-imposed burdens and your headaches will vanquish." (I suffer from migraines.) I stirred, momentarily dazed and shocked. I felt around on the covers to see if I was really awake, or if it was a dream within a dream. The brightness of the light still cast spots before my eyes, even in the darkness. I thought to myself, *if it wasn't real, then why do I have these light spots?* Then I went back into a deep sleep. I woke up the next morning with a true feeling of awe, pondering the experience and pondering it for days. The word "vanquish" kept haunting me, so I pulled out a dictionary. Magically, my index finger was pulled to a particular definition and not the first definition—"to gain mastery over." Wow! A surge of energy rippled through my body, not like lightning but waves, grateful for the divine connection and spark of healing so desperately desired. I was *awe full*.

I also realized that "vanquish" was not a normal part of my vocabulary; a clue from Jesus (Yeshua) that the experience was *absolutely* real. It was tangible. How honored, blessed, and grateful I was in that moment and still remain. My divine family cared enough to send me a message that would save me from self-destruction.

So enmeshed in self-healing, self, and ego, I did not see the greater meaning of the message: *mastering third dimension will vanquish our self-imposed burdens*. Geez, I must be stubborn. It took ten years for that to sink in. Or is that a limiting belief that I have told you not to buy into? Oui. I had to cut the wires to my programming one at a time and carefully.

Your divine family is there for you, too. Just keep talking to them and listen. When you take moments of quiet contemplation, don't judge if the answer doesn't come in that moment. You may gain recognition in a more profound way.

Where can you see, feel, hear, or notice yourself being stuck in some unconscious program? Where can you see yourself stuck in a self-imposed unconscious program? With integrity, ask yourself: Where do I complain without having implemented behavioral changes? Do I wear complaining about problems like my favorite old soft comfortable tee shirt? Have I considered that change is possible? Have I considered that my complaining is my ego's way of getting *my* attention?

Once in a while, I get caught in a complaint trap, too. My complaining usually stems from the mundane stuff around the house. Yeeaah! I am just going to blow that away with some breath—in through the nose, nice and deep...ah, that's better. Try something new. Don't try something you think is new but is really just the same old crap in another form. Going through the same motions doesn't create change. Are you willing to step out of your comfort zone?

Think you tried and nothing works? Well, suck it up and try it again. Stop saying, "I can't." Stop saying, "I can't because they won't." Practice and practice some more. Try a slightly different practice; make a small shift in the practice. Try something entirely new. Try allowing. Try saying, Yes! In today's world, there are numerous techniques. No matter what other techniques you employ, incorporating the mastery of meditation will move you towards the concept of "know thyself" and provide you with answers. Try it in a group, try it alone, try it guided, or try it walking. Try different ways of meditation and don't get stuck in just one way. Choose between the red pill and the blue pill? What a divine metaphor! Seriously, I have watched over and over to really digest the depth of that movie, knowing how many simply watch for entertainment. Which pill do you suppose the purely for entertainment and pleasure seekers chose? We all know people who have chosen the blue pill, and we must keep that in mind in dealing with them. Others have said that they, *sometimes*, wish they didn't know what they know now. This clearly expresses the truth of no turning back, but you do have a choice as to what level you want to take your consciousness to.

You choose. Let go of the self-imposed fears and take a deeper look at yourself. Deeper look at yourself? Break time! I am channeling my inner *Michael Jackson*—"Man in the Mirror." Take a break and dance with me. Feel the words in your heart as you listen and move. Feel the true rhythm of life, the heartbeat. We must stop viewing things solely from a perspective of entertainment and feel them soulfully. While you are at it, let go of any judgment of Michael. We don't know the whole story. Okay, pull up YouTube; give a listen to the power in the message.

Ooh! How did that feel?

It's hard to let go of something if you don't know what the "it" is that you want to let go of. It's not always a thing (unless you are referring to an ex, joking). It's typically an emotion. For example: Yoda in the swamp scene, which *Star Wars* movie is that? I don't know...you know the swamp scene where Luke asks Yoda something like "What's in there?" And Yoda replies, "Only what you take with you." Fear—it all boils down to fear and the fear you carry with you, no matter how great or how minute. If you want to intellectualize something then intellectualize the question, does it make sense to fear you? It only makes sense when you are using fear as an intuitive tool to either keep you out of harms' way or prevent you from causing harm. That statement includes destructive and self-destructive behavior.

Take a look at yourself and make the ***change***. ***Ooh!*** That one stays with you for a while.

I *think* you get the point of this book by now. Think! Oui! Oy! Even if you think it's all a bunch of crap right now. Maybe someday, something different will be triggered. Whether you do or don't, my intent is to plant the seed.

Seed, reminds me of an experience I would like to share. I had slipped into other dimensions in other workshops but without a deep recognition that's what happened. Now, I was in a class intentionally working with dimensions, and I was the volunteer. As I lay on the table, I *think* that I am hearing *"What's a matta you."* Some Philly Italian guy was in my head; after all that is close to where I'm from. For a while, my family lived next to an Italian restaurant. I used to sneak into the kitchen as soon as I learned to walk, and sometimes my mom would find me drinking Shirley Temples at the bar midday. I knew that what I was hearing was just a clue for me to get out of my head and not the correct message, so I honored that and dropped deeper into my heart center with breath.

At that moment, the instructor asked what was happening. I said, "Well, it's not making sense to me, so I will just say what I am hearing. I was hearing *'Watsu Maru Umu.'"*

A woman in the class popped up and said, "That's Japanese." Being of Japanese heritage, she would know! What a blessing to have someone in the class who could interpret a language that I did not know and confirm that what was happening was real. *"Watsu"* is water. We live on the water planet. *"Maru"* is a *perfect* circle. This symbol is painted on Japanese ships, with the intention that a ship returns safely home full circle from its journey. *"Umu"* is to produce, lay eggs, or be born. How about planting seeds? Message: on this water planet; return home full circle to self; your purpose is to plant seeds.

There is more. Recently, I came across a piece that I had written back in the '90s after attending a workshop hosted by Keith Varnum (check out thedream.com) that he published in his newsletter. It was precisely about planting seeds, cracking hard nuts, and letting go of the ones that I couldn't. The fact that it came to me again years later in the form of a foreign language I had no knowledge of, with an interpreter in the room, is just more evidence to me that we must hear our lessons over and over again in different forms from different sources until we get them, integrate them, and remember who we really are. My message came full spiral with no karmic repercussions attached.

As you step into consciousness, your messages will become clearer, too.

Maybe the idea of laying eggs is more profound than planting seeds as, typically, an egg starts inside the body, but a seed is outside. Dear God, that is just over thinking and something that you want to avoid.

Now is the time to deprogram and reprogram, and recreate what has been miscreated. We are being taught to come from a heart-centered consciousness, but do not disregard the value of your entire being, including your brain, your intellect, and your ego.

Making change in the world, no matter how great or how small, is that a good reason to become conscious? A really good "why bother"?

Funny thing is that I was taught to *keep my mouth shut and keep the peace*. When I would ask a question, my mom and dad would say, "What are you doing, writing a book?" This would leave me feeling bad and frustrated.

Towards the end of my dad's life, there was a surface level experience that I gained a great deal of pleasure from, which contained many opposite elements of things my dad tried to teach me. I told him, "I am getting so much pleasure out of this that I am going to spend the rest of my life doing everything the opposite of what you ever told me." We laughed.

After his passing, a random conversation sparked an interest in having a reading with a medium. Honestly, I wasn't expecting my dad to show up, but he did. In that reading, he told me to "keep my day job." At the time, this book was erupting inside me, preparing to take form. This really irritated me, and in the past it would have been enough for me to doubt what I was doing. I questioned, "How is that in alignment with spirit when spirit is telling me it is time to move on?" I suddenly realized it *is* the joke between me and my dad. This was his way of not telling but getting me to do exactly the opposite, so I would be on a path to end suffering. He is and always was quite a joker.

You see, as this book began to take form—in a waking moment before I became conscious—I heard a voice. It said, "Eight paths to suffering." *Suffering?* I thought. *That's disturbing.* These various voices are familiar, and I knew it was important. Coffee, cats, and dogs before anything else get attention. Then a simple Google search was all it took to reveal a path I was not familiar with: a Buddhist method. It was not a path to suffering, but a path to **END** suffering. The sound bite was all I needed at the moment. I knew this was the path that I was on. With this message, the message from my dad was untangled. Thank you, Dad. I love you, and I know you love me even though your ego wouldn't allow you to say it while you were here. So, now, I say: question things, question authority, question what you have been led to believe—question everything. And, yes, Dad, I am writing a book.

Chapter 2

Contradiction, Perception, Interpretation, Misinterpretation

If you have already begun a contemplative journey, I am sure there are a lot of things you are doing right. However, if you are like me and some of my playmates, there are often subtle hints or not so subtle hints that we miss. It's like we are in a constant game of hide-and-seek, but "seek and ye shall find." Song time: *Fireflight* – "Desperate".

We live in a world of contradiction. We live in a world of opposites. We live in this world of right, wrong, good, bad, your way, my way, and the highway, too much, not enough, never enough, higher, lower, in between, left, right, wrong, correct, light, dark, deep, shallow, easy, hard, overwhelming, and not so bad. *It can be quite maddening*. Was that me or Morpheus? Both!

We have this perception of ever reaching higher that higher is always better when we often find peace at sea level while listening to gentle yet powerful waves. So what is this "higher level" we are labeling and reaching for? It's vibration. Since thoughts and words have vibration, it is important for us to consider the way we perceive and express. Particularly consider how the way we express affects us and others. How often do we use expressions out of habit but haven't really pondered the meaning of the expression ourselves? Sure sayings have a time and a place but many are misused. How often have we heard the expression "You can't have it both ways"? Or "You can't have your cake and eat it, too?" What a great way to make you feel unworthy when used in the wrong context. It's like dangling a carrot in front of a horse. It's just mean.

Regardless of the intended meaning, there is a definitive undertone of limiting belief. Of course, once you eat that piece of cake, you can't have it anymore, because it's gone. But that doesn't mean that's all there is or you shouldn't bake another cake. This type of expression is designed to keep us in suppression. Of course, we don't want to hold onto possessions for the sake of possessions either. Possessions, hmm, I'm hearing a little *Sting;* "If You Love Somebody."

The truth is how can we not have it both ways when duality is the nature of our existence? It also points to the "why bother" of being a victim of the sound bite and misinterpreting messages.

Consider opposites and opposite ends of the spectrum. In a message I was given through a channeled reading, I was told to embrace the full spectrum of Martha. Initially this may sound like b.s. and you may experience resistance but I recommend embracing the full spectrum of you. It's our job to break the program, crack the code, free ourselves from the shackles, and not just see but enjoy the full spectrum of beauty that life has to offer. It will lead to the mastery of third dimension.

Let's take a different look at both sides of the spectrum. Playing in the full spectrum will allow us to enjoy the breaks and rests at any point along the way. To achieve appreciation, we need diverse experiences. It's difficult to understand what a feeling is without experiencing its opposite. So you might have to experience a little sadness to know what joy is. That doesn't mean that we can't have our cake and enjoy eating it. You might get little nibbles along the way until someday life offers you a whole piece. Sometimes you will taste something you don't like. So what? It's just an experience. Sometimes we learn through the process of elimination. There is a difference between an uncomfortable choice and stepping out of your comfort zone. Be clear on that. You don't have to do anything that is completely uncomfortable when your intuition tells you that something just isn't right. While you are taking taste tests, playing both sides and the middle allow yourself to recognize the diversity and say viva la difference.

In this world we live in, we are all subject to contradiction and consistency, perception and misperception, interpretation and misinterpretation. So it is understandable that if we are all creators, we will miscreate from time to time.

If you focus on the fear of making wrong choices, you are denying yourself experiences. Remember, that while making a choice not to do something may open the possibility of something better coming along, you do not want to be in a state of perpetual wait. When something feels natural, explore it. Explore what natural feels like to you. Sit back, rest and observe when it feels natural. You don't have to do what feels unnatural, unless doing something unnatural helps you to break the program that has kept you out of your natural world. On the other hand, jumping at every opportunity without considering if it feels natural is a fear of missing out. So ask yourself: *What am I really going to miss? Will this experience enhance or enrich my life? Will this experience bring me joy?* Sometimes we don't know the reason why we want to do something; we just feel drawn. That may be enough, and the reason may or may not reveal itself later. There may come a time when you go, *Oh yeah, now I get it. Geez, that was years ago.* Even if you experience disappointment, there is a lesson in there and something to be grateful for. Again, the lesson and the gratitude may not reveal itself until later, so just accept the disappointment as an experience for something greater to come. But be open to allowing the greater to come.

We have this perception that reaching further is better when there are *some things* that serve us just as well that are right in front of us. If we don't see them, it is a misperception. This is not necessarily *our perception*, because there is no ownership in misperceiving. Accountability; yes, but ownership; no. Sometimes we need to take another look, a deeper look; look at things from another perspective or another vantage point. I understand that you will only

15

achieve what it is you strive for, so set the bar high. I understand we often have greater appreciation for that which we have worked harder for. However, there is value in *awareness* and appreciating the things that have been set before us. This is how we allow ourselves the opportunity to have things both ways. Don't forget to ask to have your third eye opened to see, hear, feel, notice and enjoy with more clarity.

When you look around, it's obvious that it's important to make some corrections to the way we perceive and proceed. While things change, there is still a lot of the same shit, different day. Too often we place value on small things and forget to look at the bigger picture, while at other times, we forget that the little details can be important. What does that mean? It means that in the interconnected, intertwined universe we live in every day, everything is important; everything has relevance. Everything is important, and, at the same time, nothing is more important than how we perceive our world. We need to care more, but we also need to care less. Forget the trivial but appreciate simplicity. We have to work in cooperation within the contradictions to free ourselves from the burdens of this harsh world. Cooperation doesn't mean conforming.

Since we live in this world of contradiction, it's no wonder that we misinterpret things. In accepting that we *will* misinterpret along the way, there is a *value* in misinterpretation *in that*, when we get *it*, we will finally master the lesson.

Often we misinterpret because we are allowing the ego to be in control. If we could all learn to read, write, speak, listen and communicate in any form from the heart center, there would be a lot less conflict and a lot more understanding. We also misinterpret due to a lack of knowledge and information or direct personal experience. So do not be afraid of any experience that potentially opens your heart, your mind, your soul however you want to label "it." The opening creates freedom. Freedom creates peace and vice versa. In choosing to build walls, you are miscreating your life.

Sometimes you can't see things from another person's perspective unless they are willing to share it with you, nor will they see it from yours unless you are willing to share it with them, which is the only pathway to create understanding. Without the ability to clearly express from an integrated heart center, which includes the ego being in check, we must accept the possibility that understanding might be difficult, if not impossible, in this lifetime to achieve. That doesn't mean <u>we</u> should not attempt to see things from someone else's perspective.

It's a fairly safe bet that I will contradict myself somewhere in this book, and a misunderstanding will be miscreated. In the meantime, I hear *The Police's* "Wrapped Around Your Finger" echoing how art imitates life, and life imitates art.

As humans, we are expressive creatures by nature. Consider that letting go of limiting beliefs allows us to express more freely. How does the idea of freedom make you feel? Good, right? Now, I don't want to take anything away from that feeling, but freedom doesn't mean being irresponsible. Why? Because: we are responsible for our freedom. Sometimes we are stuck between a *rock and a hard place*, but we can make choices that let go of drama and allow us to feel at peace even if that means standing up for peace. How often do you find yourself pursing your lips or clenching your jaw? That's your body's way of asking you to check in with you heart center.

Everything is subject to interpretation. In this case, using a definitive third-dimensional term applies. Maybe someday it won't, but for now, *everything* we see, hear, think, feel, and perceive is subject to interpretation. Can we learn to interpret from a non-ego, non-emotional perspective? Sure, why not. Perhaps instead of non-ego, non-emotional, it would better serve to state that you *can* learn to view differently, perceive differently, and interpret differently if you know how to be more heart-centered, aligned with spirit, aligned with ego, aligned with fearlessness, aligned with being limitless, aligned with divine connection. By this, you *will* learn to interpret from a broader, more expanded different perspective. The latter not only sounds better, but it feels better. But would it have the same impact if your ability hadn't been questioned first?

Everyone has their own perception, and we perceive and interpret from our viewpoint. No one else is in our head or precisely knows what we are thinking. No one else can truly read your mind. We could all learn to communicate better. Do we sometimes know others well enough to intuitively know exactly what they are thinking? Sure. Can we read a person's expression and have a good idea of what's going on in there? Sure, especially if we know someone intimately. It can be fun when we know someone so well that we agree without words. That's intimacy. Go ahead; remember one of those experiences now. I bet it brings a smile to your face. On the other hand, it can be quite annoying when we know that you are reading the body language of opposition. But forget about that right now. Go back to that smile.

There are genuine psychics that do a good job reading your energy, but they really don't know everything and don't expect them to. They are people, too, with many of the same challenges we all have. Cracks me up when someone naively goes to a psychic and *fears* that he/she knows everything; like the "great and powerful Oz." Come on; let's use a little common sense. While psychics have an ability, that does not mean they are more powerful than you. Some are genuine, some are charlatans, some can offer assistance, but none of them know you intimately, unless your friend *is* the psychic. *It's not all about you.* It is a good idea for you to get to know yourself intimately and surprise yourself with your own power of what you know.

Why do some of us go to psychics anyway? Perhaps it is impatience. Perhaps it is desperation. Perhaps it is curiosity. However, when you are given messages that don't show up in your time frame, that doesn't mean the messages were wrong. That's could be your misinterpretation. That's why you can't rely on the information or use it as a crutch.

A good psychic (Glinda, the good witch) can give you messages, but you have to check in with your heart to *in*terpret them and *im*plement a strategy for any good advice to come to fruition. Use the messages they provide as a tool, not as gospel. Since we are on the topic of psychic, knowing is not the same as predicting. You have free will. If a psychic starts to *tell* you what to do, you need to heed that as a warning. A good reader will offer encouragement and offer caution as suggestions. They only tell you what they see and hear, not always what they know. Messages are always more powerful when they come from your intimate, internal, intuitive knowing.

Your perception comes from the way you perceive your experiences, which comes in the form of lessons. Even a pleasant experience is a lesson in experiencing what pleasant feels like. Until a spiritual message or concept is integrated into your being, so your self-defeating perceptions will change, the message or lesson likely will be repeated. Even when you forget that you are always connected to the oneness or even if you intentionally or unintentionally created a disconnect, our primary goal is to master third dimension, be in oneness, and find our way back to the light. It has been said that we are "spiritual beings having human experiences, not human beings having spiritual experiences. That stuck with me from the very first time I heard it. I got it from *Wayne Dyer*. It's been credited to *Pierre Teilhard de Chardin*. Who is he? I don't know, but something tells me we should pay attention to that sound bite since he appears to have been on to something important.

We are all here with our own unique perspective. Perspective always changes throughout life. We choose to what degree and how wide of a spectrum we wish to embrace. "Always" in this case is not a definitive term, but refers to *all ways*. If you take "always" as definitive, this is where you latch on to limitations.

To evolve, we want to let go of some of the finite perspective. Since everything has a relationship, it would serve to know exactly what it is that we are trying to communicate. Although it doesn't always come out right or is not received right, saying what you mean and meaning what you say is the best that you can do, as long as you get your ego out of the way and speak from the heart. When you learn to speak from your heart, you will begin to be more comfortable in your own skin. That doesn't mean that exercising your intuition won't have uncomfortable moments.

Everything in life has energy. Everything has vibration. We have vibration. Words have vibration. So our words have more profound impact on our lives than we often chose to recognize. In third dimension and our current scientific understanding, we describe vibration and frequency as higher or lower. It's fairly simple to understand. It is also safe to say that as you raise your vibration, you may notice that your life flows more effortlessly. However, in these earthly bodies, we can still fall on our faces as we learn to dance to the rhythm. Noticing where we tripped is the job of the observer who, in turn, rings the bell of the conscious self. "Ring My Bell" (*Anita Ward*), now that might not be your style but that was a great dance tune in its day and reminds me of learning to let go and have fun when I believed "I (only) love rock and roll" (made famous by *Joan Jett &The Blackhearts*).

Deepak (being a rock star of the metaphysical world and needing no last name anymore) does a brilliant exercise in experiencing participation and awareness. I *think* it was 1998 (the difference between thinking and knowing has no value here) when I got to see him in a large hall in Philly. He asked the whole audience to put their attention on themselves, and then asked the audience to put their attention on him. Wow! If you couldn't feel that shift in energy, I think you were probably dead. Who knows, maybe it was Deepak's way of stealing energy since all the attention was on him. Kidding! Please don't sue me for slander. I think he is brilliant, and he *definitely* has moved my molecules of perception toward truth even when it pissed me off.

This leads to explain a little more about the commonly misunderstood concept—being the observer. I am including it here and not in the chapter of things that pissed me off, because it didn't piss me off. I just didn't get it at first. When I was first told to practice being the observer, I immediately thought, *Why would I want to be an observer? Don't I want to have my own experiences? Isn't going through life as an observer like being a robot? Who wants to be a wallflower, worse yet, a fly on the wall, yuk? Isn't going through life as an observer and detaching from my emotion a form of suppressing my emotions? Isn't that just another form of denial? Isn't part of the experience and part of the uniqueness of being human about having emotions? Aren't aliens trying to figure out how to be more human? How the heck does being an observer make any sense?* My ego had fun coming up for excuses to resist, but, geek moment, resistance was futile.

The purpose of the observer state is a tool to help you detach long enough from belief, emotion and ego, guiding you to a heart-based, rational, logical place where you can observe what is occurring or what did occur, so that you can make new, more practical choices from a clear conscious perspective in <u>cooperation</u> with your head (your crown and you third eye), so you can communicate clearly with your voice (throat chakra) using discernment (high heart) to bridge any gaps. It doesn't mean you live as the observer. The observer is another aspect of you. It could be stated that the observer is the yin to the yang of the ego or vice versa. The observer can get those angels sitting on each shoulder to agree. How often is it easier for someone else to see something going on with us that we can't see ourselves? Or how often can we see what is going on with someone else? Utilizing our own personal observer stops us from being a busy body or from being tripped up by one. Detaching is not an excuse to become aloof. There are some attachments we want to keep.

Observation leads to comprehension, which leads to coping, but once we do that, we may want to ask the observer, if we are ready to drop some of the armor around our heart, which will ultimately lead to amore (love).

Initially, in learning about heart-centered consciousness, I began to blame my head for everything. I know others who blamed their brain and thinking process as well, which is why I feel it is so important to share. Often you will hear those in the new age and metaphysical community say, "Just come from your heart and stop thinking." I blamed my thought process for everything. Funny, because my dad always said, "Use your head," or "You got a brain, use it." Now, all of a sudden, all these people are telling me to stop using my head and use my heart. Dear God, help me figure this out! In fact, I recall a time when we were told not to think with our heart, because it could lead us astray. Of course that usually is thinking with another body part and not really our hearts, if you know what I mean.

There is a bit of a communication breakdown here. While we still don't know everything about our mind/brain connection and while the debate continues, obviously there is a direct relationship to our intellect. Our ability to think, process information, rationalize and use common sense is primarily a function of the brain, but it isn't separate from the rest of your body. If our brain isn't functioning we are brain dead. While common sense is sorely lacking, there can be times when common sense is merely an opinion, so it would appear we need to develop a rapport with our discernment and stop knocking the thinking process. Maybe instead of just peering into the window of our soul, we should be knocking on all the closed doors within ourselves and say "hello, is anyone home?"

Maybe I should take back what I said about the number one problem in combining a spiritual world with everyday life—over-intellectualizing and over-thinking spirituality. Maybe we are underthinking or maybe we aren't thinking at all. How many times do we observe a situation and say, *what were they thinking?* How can we learn to come from the heart if we don't think about coming from the heart? This is why integration of all parts will create greater harmony.

How do you know you have been overthinking unless you experience what happens when you over think? This is why learning to know what you know and knowing what knowing feels like is more appropriate in our evolution. Knowing is an integration of our thinking and our feeling emanating from the heart-center.

When we get hung up in the judgment, which comes from incorrect thinking, it creates a disconnect en route to our heart center. Our heart allows us to express more kindly, gently, and compassionately. When we let go of the judgment, our heart and head can begin to communicate and cooperate in harmony. There is an exchange that goes on between the head and the heart or the heart and the head when we are in present moment awareness, which is not mutually exclusive. Learning to communicate without judgment is the path to overcome injustice.

Keep in mind that overthinking and doubt also contain elements of judgment. Pay more attention to your self-defeating self-talk and idle chatter; these things are what will get you in trouble. Wait! Correction! Don't pay more attention to those things that might get you stuck. Just notice them. Notice patterns and change the energy around what you are doing that is less than ideal, and solutions will be more easily found. Your mind and your brain are not the same thing, yet they are not mutually exclusive either.

Learn to breathe and drop into your heart. Life itself begins and ends with heartbeat and breath and the reason why all meditative practices use breath. The breath allows us to drop into the heart-center, gifting us in knowing when we have reached the place we choose to be. However, it's a good idea to be *mindful* and to practice *mindfulness* while we are practicing being heart-centered. Again, it's the idea of integrating the head and the heart and the rest of our being that will help us achieve consciousness.

Your high heart is the place of discerning the difference between thinking and knowing. It's not always recognized, because it is not considered one of the seven main chakras. I have come to know this area between the heart and the throat as that place where the gap is bridged. Knowing comes with a sense of peace and sovereignty, as if a place where two points converge. If there is sense of peace and sovereignty, it's "all systems go"; if not, "Houston, we have a problem." Check in with the heart center until everyone is in agreement. Yes, I said everyone. Ask which voices need to be honored and which one need to be told to shut up. Consult with your high council inside of you and outside of you. Negotiate until you reach a peace treaty, so you can express authentically.

Ask your heart for an agreement as to which thoughts are beliefs and which thoughts are what you know to be the truth. Use the high-heart bridge to get you there. Oh, and be cautious of the ego-troll underneath the bridge. When harmony is reached, even the ego has no choice but to sit in the audience, shut up, and enjoy the show.

To achieve mastery, it is suggested that we learn to slow the idle chatter in our thinking brain and put to rest the thoughts that hold us back. Learn to feel using the heart as the headquarters where thoughts are placed under a cone of silence until they are discerned.

In learning to discern, we recognize our programming and conditioning. The new process of dismissing from service old concepts, such as fear, judgment, disappointment, anger, and lack will begin to be replaced with new concepts, such as cooperation, abundance, harmony, and joy, ultimately leading to unconditional love. Be patient. Let the order of the issues wanting to be released come up naturally. Let go of expectation. There are things that have been hidden even from you. As you allow thoughts and programs to surface naturally, they will more easily dissolve and lead you to resolve. Unconditional love will start to appear only when the old programs stop running in the background.

Now, this leads me to grounding. Boots on the ground! Every war needs ground troops. Right? Remember, it is the inner war that creates the outer war. War exists in each of us to varying degrees. If every government around the planet would start to understand this and let go of ego, the whole world would become whole. We must remember that the government is just the thing. It is people, often misguided people, who are running the show. Imagine if we had an ego meter to test someone before they ever throw their hat into the ring; the ring being the karmic circle of destruction.

I am not saying we will or we won't self-destruct. But why would we even want to test that possibility? Why is humanity so fixated on war? Is our perception of humanity that warped? I find it so baffling and painful that sometimes I don't think I am really from here. "War! What is it good for? Absolutely nothin'!" ("War"-performed by *Edwin Starr*)

Wake up, look around, and weigh the options. "Bomb the World" (*Michael Franti*)? A distinct possibility? No joke. "(What's so Funny 'Bout) Peace, Love, and Understanding" (*Elvis Costello*)? "Imagine" (*John Lennon*) that peace exists. Let's stop just imagining. Why wouldn't we want to <u>do</u> everything in our power to stop war and hate? Power does not have to mean force. We have to choose if we want to be part of the self-destructive cycle or if we want to break it and help create something more peaceful. The possibility of self-destruction exists in each of us. But guess what. So does the possibility of peace! Peace could be a reality if we were all more grounded in consciousness.

On the flipside, some may say, if I am always grounded, how can I learn to expand into possibilities and other dimensions? Don't people achieve enlightenment with out of body experiences? At the risk of sounding judgmental, it's just not something I recommend. My experience is that once you fully understand what it feels like to be grounded, heart-centered, and divinely connected at the same time, our experiences are more profound, because these elements create present-moment awareness and mindfulness.

Living in denial from a trauma or any other fear you don't want to face takes you out of your body unconsciously. It doesn't have to be a huge fear. You may be so far into denial that you deny being in denial. Leaving your body is an avoidance technique, and you may not even know you are doing it. I can hear some say, "Leave my body." What the heck is she talking about? If you are regularly experiencing distraction, suffering from chaos, drama, illness, and injury, particularly in shorter segments, you are probably not grounded. It's very difficult to heal, become whole, and exercise discernment, unless your spirit is connected to your body and grounded. There is more to long term suffering, but it does not discount the need for grounding.

If we are here on earth to have human experiences, it's really hard to master something when you are walking around with your head in the clouds. Just sayin'.

Grounding is a feeling that you will get to know through awareness. Make it your friend. Find a facilitator, find a class, or a partner and practice. We may be able to win an outer war with an army of *300*; the inner war only takes one. Grounding may help with your stability and ability to feel love and not just the idea of love but really feel love.

Do we crave love even if we don't want to admit it? Yes. But, as *Pee Wee* would say, "There's always a big but." But there is so much misperception around the idea of unconditional love. With all our third-dimensional beliefs, particularly limits and judgment, it's hard to comprehend the idea that unconditional love exists. Loving unconditionally does not mean you have to be a doormat! Loving unconditionally does not mean you must stay in a relationship that is toxic. Loving unconditionally does not mean you allow unacceptable behavior to perpetuate. Loving unconditionally doesn't make it okay to be an enabler. Self-love does not mean being selfish. Self-love when not selfish is completely acceptable and appropriate in mastery of what we came here to do. Staying in an abusive relationship because someone told you that to love God is to love others unconditionally makes no sense whatsoever when it would serve God, you, your soul, and others more greatly to let go of all fear around stepping into personal power and independence. Muster the strength and the courage to move on. The pain in doing so is only temporary. Love always returns in another form if you allow it.

I recall in the very first workshop I attended on learning to come from a heart-centered consciousness, Keith Varnum said, *one of the hardest things we may do is to let go of people in our lives.* Namaste to you, Keith Varnum! You master in human form! There was a profound truth in those words. It was something I desperately needed to do. His words gave me great strength and courage. Letting go can sometimes be painful, but we can come through the experiences unscathed and unscarred, unlike what occurs while we are attached.

Letting go doesn't have to mean totally cutting off any relationship, unless you want to. Accept that some may cut you out. Don't take it personal. Some people like their toxicity and can't handle your higher vibration. Relationships will change in many ways, distance, disappearance, dissolution, and detachment. Watch the detached relationship because those are usually the ones who treat us like detainees—the button pushers. You know, the ones who, no matter how well we do while not in their presence and no matter how much we shrink our buttons, the buttons will explode massively at the first word out of their mouth, like stepping on a land mine. Suddenly, you begin to feel dizzy, sick to the stomach, that you want to just run away screaming. Remember to breathe; don't hyperventilate. Know that you are loved in the world outside of this place. In this scenario, we really need to call on our integrity and learn to forgive them while remembering not to expect them to notice that you are changing for the better.

"Blessed are the birds of the field, they do not sow yet they reap." You might think you have worked hard to change so you deserve to reap and can't possibly be the bird in this scenario. But guess what. You just might be the bird. *The others* sow all right, and you reap their havoc. No wonder the expression is actually wreaking havoc. These sowers seem to flourish from the havoc they have wrecked upon you. This is a really good "why bother" for us to stop the power failure we let them create. It's too painful. Trust that at some time and place, if you remain in integrity, even if they see you as less than who you really are and see you as a bad guy, your determination to change will help you find a much better home. You may need to live in a fortress for a while, but don't lock yourself up in the tower permanently. The reward you reap from taking your power back will greatly outweigh anything that you leave behind.

Fortress has come up more than once and I can't hold back any longer. It's time for *Sting's* "Fortress around Your Heart." Breathe and enjoy.

We all know that running away doesn't solve anything. When you do, you just get the same issue in a different time, place, and form. So, if you really want to change, stop running away; accept that you chose this life. If you simply need a do over, that's one thing, but doing it over and over without change is insanity. I understand the desire to evolve, and I agree that some things can be done out of order. But the fact is you are here to find a degree of acceptance. Degree—hmm, degree of acceptance and mastery without a hefty price tag.

None of us want to live in a space of anger, but damning the world to hell and wanting to get off this planet is not living in the present. The desire to run away could just be a lesson in patience or a push to persevere. Maybe the pain you have experienced is so deep that the fortress covers more than just your heart. If you aren't ready to start to feel in your heart, you may need to start lower into your solar plexus, sacral chakra, root chakra or maybe even below your feet, until you begin to feel something. You might discover passion wanting to rise up. Let it.

If time heals all wounds, and time and space are connected, you may possibly just need space. There is a difference between taking yourself out of a toxic environment where you can heal and running away. How many times can you let yourself be stabbed in the heart before you say, enough is enough? If this is the case, then you are not running away. You are just taking care of yourself and learning to create a new life and new home in yourself that is healthy. Just be cautious that you have learned what you needed to learn about the toxicity, so it doesn't show up in your life again. If it does, hopefully, it only shows up as a temporary reminder of just how far you have come and gone and will leave just as quickly.

Let's try it with breath; sense the opposites. This is how far I've come. That's how far I've gone. If you know where you want to be allow the breath to say, *This is where I am, and that's where I want to be.* If you are uncertain, let breath show you possibilities as it is breath that creates a true sense of power and encouragement for going the distance.

Certainly, by now we've all heard the expression "lose your fears." Back around 1988, my primary guide revealed himself to me on a different level of reality than what is commonly perceived as reality even though that veil is lifting. We already know that in the linear past, many of us would have been locked up, drugged (oh, that still happens), stoned, or otherwise put to death for having a different perception of reality, especially speaking to beings without physical form. But let's not talk about the martyr archetype here. I used to call that one the Marthyr paradigm since I was deeply rooted in it. I've always accused my mother of having the martyr program. I was so embarrassed when I discovered it was also in me. Not. I just had to work hard at plucking it out. Dang it, I said let's not talk about that.

It's crazy how the church, and our parents teach that we all have a guardian angel, but if you see and talk to yours, it's imaginary. Huh? I wonder if God used imagination before he created us. Magic Cloud is my guardian angel. To meet him, to come to know him by name, and have him provide clues to who he was/is, is an extraordinary honor in my story. I wish every being on this planet would share this type of experience, and they can if they allow it. They walk among us and need not be feared. However, if you are living in fear, be wary of the deception that exists. Our true guides, guardian angels, often stay in the background, because they are here to protect us and help us grow up. They aren't codependent upon us and don't want us to be codependent on them.

I have felt Magic Cloud's intervention at work. He provided a spark of trust when I had difficulty trusting anyone or anything. One of the first things Magic Cloud said to me was, "*Lose your fears.*" Of course, I interpreted that as the power of positive thinking. I believed that all I had to do was think positive and everything would be rosy my way. Problem was that I hadn't learned to discern or trust my gut instincts or intuition. I let go, all right, but I did not take proper precautions when intuition told me to. So while positive thoughts create a world of possibility, we still might want to stop judging negative. Negative gets a bad rap when it serves to help us see negative circumstance and to see that we are not necessarily using the power of the positive in the correct context. Learn to discern. Let go of the right fears. Let go of the fears that hold you back. Just because you are given a message does not mean that you do not have a lesson to go along with the message.

Pretty much through this whole section, I kept hearing *The Animals,* "Don't Let Me Be Misunderstood." Yes, it fits. Give it a listen while you do ask yourself, *Where do I feel misunderstood? Where am I not offering understanding? Can I embrace misunderstanding and allow understanding to enter my life? What would that feel like if I did?*

Chapter 3

Things That Pissed Me Off
When I Misinterpreted Them

E ven though we already know that we often learn more from our mistakes than we do when we get it right the first time, how many times have you said to yourself, *I'm never doing that again*? On the other hand, how many times do we say to ourselves, *When will I ever learn?* Yeah, well, we learn some things quicker than others, some lessons are deeper. Sometimes the element of hope wins, and sometimes things appear hopeless and it's time to let go. Let's get one thing straight, we overuse the word "just". By saying "just let go", the ego misinterprets that as a dismissal of feelings or feels like it is being judged because we haven't already let go, even if that is not the intent of the statement. Letting go is a choice that we need to keep our ego out of. Developing discernment and intuition are our guiding factors in learning to pursue and persevere.

We've all been annoyed or downright pissed off at some point, and trauma can create deep anger, which, if we can learn to embrace, we can learn to move past. Learning just to handle something, or to cope, keeps you stuck in coping and the past. And it keeps you in a cycle where whatever it is you are feeling keeps returning. Anger comes in varying degrees like all emotions and can burn pretty bad the hotter it gets. Some things just take longer to cool down than others. Sometimes that low-level anxiety you may be experiencing is either a way to control what you are feeling without fully facing what is inside and under the surface or a method of outright denial.

This points to the "why bother" that we have to hear a lesson over and over until we finally start to "get it," and sometimes we just don't know what we just don't know. To experience change, we have to observe our behavior and be willing to make changes.

As you can imagine, our best lessons come from things that piss us off even when we deny being angry. We tend to place more value and appreciation on lessons that are the most difficult. So when you find yourself with lots of emotional attachments, you best put your boots on and make sure they are made for mucking, because you are going to be walking in some shit. Here are a few things that pissed me off before I discovered what was really pissing me off.

Number One Piss Me Off: All illness is a manifestation of emotion.

So, the first time that I heard *Deepak Chopra* say, "All illness is a manifestation of emotion," my reaction was, *How dare he say that. There is pollution and pesticide-laden food. What about genetics and birth defects? How can children create cancer? Nuclear reactors, dioxin, endocrine disruptors in our environment, birds and fish are dying, and the horses won't drink from the stream anymore; they snort at the water.* We weren't even talking about GMOs back then. I was quite agitated. *What bullshit*, I thought. Although nothing is only one way in this world of duality, I do see the truth in what he said. At the time, I was still running the victim program. My ego still wanted to bond on "woundology," as *Caroline Myss* would say. Had you asked me, I would have denied that my ego came in to play, I would have denied playing the victim, and I would have denied that I liked to bond on wounds.

There are those who have studied the connectedness of certain types of illness, disease, and physical weakness in relation to certain emotional traumas. It's true; we store emotions in our bodies. Cancer, indigestion, weak knees, shoulder problems, neck pain (a pain in the neck), sciatic pain (a pain in the ass), injury, you name it—comes from some emotional experience or perceived trauma that you had. It's all a setup to experience something. If you have been injured by someone else, regardless if it is physically or emotionally, you may have chosen to learn about the victim program, judgment, shame, and the opposites, support, courage, the list goes on. But there is a lesson and mastery involving accepting both sides of the story. Since it's never too late to learn, understanding this may create a sense of peace and acceptance, especially if this physical body is about to "Give Up the Ghost" (*Radiohead*).

Even though I didn't know what I was doing back then, somehow, someway, no matter how pissed off or annoyed I was, I stuck with some of these concepts and began to see the connections. Somewhere in my heart and knowing, I could feel the truth of what I was hearing and made a conscious choice to ride it out and not give up, until I was able to come to a peaceful realization of this truth. Truth is even in knowing what I know, there are still things that annoy me. But that is only because I don't have a full comprehension of the lesson that *I chose* to master, and my ego gets impatient. However, the more we recognize and learn to work with our egos, the easier it becomes. And we begin to see the importance of healing from multiple aspects—physically, mentally, emotionally and intellectually. It's all energy, and we must learn how to process all aspects of the energy to be whole.

So what triggers you? What makes you annoyed? What makes you dizzy? What makes you feel ill? Are you sick and tired of feeling sick and tired, angry, annoyed, or frustrated? Are you willing to look at illness and pain from an inside perspective so you can learn to embrace them and let them go?

Which leads me to another subject that pissed me off: how the heck can I be the creator of everything? Talk about setting up a program.

Number Two Piss Me Off: Creation—
You create everything.

There is this idea that we create everything; we create our reality. There is truth in that, to a great extent. Psalms 82:6 says we are all gods (small "g"). This belief stems from *we were created by God, so we are god*. Jesus said something similar: "the God that is within me is within you."

There is a common question when someone learns about being a creator; Why would I create this? This is where the big *piss me off* came in. When we find ourselves in deep crap, we find it hard to believe that we would choose to create certain experiences. We find ourselves emphatically stating, "There is *no way* I would choose to create this." Why would I create illness, sadness, disappointment, or heartbreak? Why wouldn't I just choose to win the lottery? Having a Catholic background, I wasn't worthy of being a creator. You don't have to be Catholic. A major portion of the planet has to been conditioned to believe they are unworthy and not even know they have that belief. Can you relate?

Then there is: "Well, if I created it, then it must be my fault, I am responsible for *everything*. If I created it, then some part of me must have asked for it. I did this to myself. God must be punishing me; the devil is after me. I'm a sinner." Talk about guilt, shame, blame, feeling unworthy, worthless, stupid, embarrassed, wanting to crawl into a hole and just die. What a load of crap! Add to that your own memory or image of an authority figure in your life who said the words, "You asked for it," and—bam!—what recipe for self-imposed loathing that is, even when our heart and intellect tells us this self-talk is pointless. The ideal choice is to vanquish all those false perceptions.

The more awake we become, the louder the bells, whistles and alarms get, the red flags pop up faster and we are able to more ideally create our true heart's desires from an integrated soul level. What we can't change becomes more acceptable from the standpoint that we can accept that whatever happened, had happened, not that what happened is a morally, ethically, spiritually acceptable behavior or circumstance. Be aware of the multiple interpretations of words, especially accept and acceptable.

Of course, we all know those who are never responsible; it's never their fault; it's always someone else's fault; someone else "should" do something. It's easy for the givers in the world to fall into the trap of the takers. Part of awakening is paying attention to your participation.

Until we recognize that we are not solely responsible and simply recognize our soul's role, more self-talk shows up: *If I created it, then why can't I just uncreate it? I want a do over. Crap, what a mess I created. I don't know how I am going to get out of this one? I am so embarrassed. I deserve to suffer. I deserve to die. I hate myself. I am so stupid.* Shut up! Stop it! Instead, start examining possibilities by considering what it is that your soul is trying to show you. Wow, the ego is a good teacher. The ego can be a trickster, but it also has a good side. The ego has taken too much bashing, just like men and women have taken too much bashing from each other. Stop bashing and stop bashing creation, good or bad, and step into integrity. Integrity comes from integration and through integration comes integrity. We can simply learn to recognize that whatever happened, had happened, not to trivialize anything, but to offer us the option to awaken, and recreate our reality.

The truth is that you came here to have human experiences, so remember that includes experiencing opposite ends of the spectrum. With creation comes miscreation. Miscreation is simply a mistake. Pick a scene and give yourself another take or cut it from the story altogether. Keep in mind that there is also co-creation and free will. If you are a creator, than so are we all. If we are to consider being open; open-minded, open-hearted, open to possibility; than we should also consider the possibility of random occurrence while acknowledging synchronicity. We live in duality. How can there not be both? To think there is only random occurrence or only synchronicity is a judgment.

If we are all connected how can we not be affected by someone else's creation? This is why it is important to create and maintain integrity by considering how our words and actions (expression) affect others.

Sometimes we are caught off guard and end up being negatively affected by someone else's creation. We are then left wondering *what the hell!* Through practice of heart-centered awareness and integrity without ego-based responses these situations are much easier to maneuver through. It is wise to remember we always have a choice as to how we participate and that mastery of third dimension involves breaking the karmic cycle of drama and destruction we have been playing in. In order to break unpleasant cycles, you may experience creations that are less than beautiful.

Now we know, not only is there creation and miscreation but there is co-creation but also co-miscreation. Allow the ego to take over and take control, or allow your authentic self to shine through and be in command. (*Collective Soul*–"Shine") The right choices are inside of you- the next piss me off.

Number Three Piss Me Off: All your answers are inside you; you already have all the answers.

Have any of you found yourself in the position of saying, "Seriously, I created this big mess, and now I am supposed to already know how to fix it." WTFH! "Come on, I know I am not that stupid! Oh, God, I must be." You might find yourself embarrassed and possibly saying, "I can't do this anymore."

You may think it's easier to stay asleep or go back to sleep (spiritually speaking). You may think it's easier to wear rose colored glasses, it's easier to turn a deaf ear, it's easier to ignore, it's easier to be numb, it's easier to turn your back, it's easier to take a pill or it's easier to forget. Do you really believe all those ways of expressing denial are the best way to find answers and create more ideally?

Sure, everyone needs a break from this mad world, but, we *all* have choices, free will, and create our own reality. Have you considered that denial is just another form of fear? Have you considered that by facing the fear it's possible that honest answers will reveal themselves? If you faced the truth, what is the very worst that could happen? Denial takes away your power. The truth while possibly causing temporary pain, always makes you stronger. It's always your choice; face the truth and in be charge of your own power source or stay in denial and allow someone else to be in control of the power that is rightfully yours.

The reality is that it feels kind of unfair, like dirty warfare, to say to someone, "All your answers are inside you," without any preface or clear understanding regardless of the truth in the statement. Though unintentional, this is sound bite victimization.

We all have answers inside of us. When we work with consciousness, we are empowered by waking up to the memory of who we really are. Waking up is a process. All answers are not revealed immediately upon comprehending the idea of waking up. It is still a journey. There are many examples of what can happen if we push anything too hard. So, the idea is to allow the journey to unfold naturally. Yes, we are empowered by coming up with our own answers and our own solutions. Having someone else provide you with answers takes your power away and does not provide you with the responsibility of doing your own work or the reward that comes with that. You are the chief; the people outside of you are the chieftains. What happens when we get our answers? I've regularly heard the comment that *we have to ask the universe*. Well guess what when you get your answers, you might also have to step up and act upon your answer.

Providing someone else with answers is like the story of the butterfly that was deformed because the man thought he was being helpful and opened the cocoon. If you haven't heard it or read about it, it's on the Internet, so it must be true. Yes that was a joke. The story helps to make sense out of the necessity for you to come up with your own answers, empowering your spiritual growth. You must find your own answers and go through your own struggles to be whole, complete, and healthy. But, it is still a metaphor; butterflies don't interact with one another the same way we do.

Be patient with the answers. If you give up, that's the ego giving up. Resist being too attached to the outcome but if you are attached, it's part of the experience of understanding how that works. See, hear, feel, notice, or allow the answers to come. Being patient allows the answers to come at just the right moment or opportunity. Stop for a moment and see if you can remember a time when you were impatient and disappointed in not getting an answer when you expected it, and then suddenly a whole new opportunity presented itself that you were grateful for. Pay attention to your opportunities. Find the smallest thing to be grateful for.

You may find yourself saying, "Why, God, why? Why is this happening to me?" Then the begging starts. "Please, please, God, help me." It's like you are clinging on to God's leg like a spoiled whiny child. You know, the ones you see in a store who can't have some crappy toy that will break the second he/she gets in the car. Thing is we all have a breaking point—a feeling of being at the end of your rope. This is exactly the place where you must find faith and courage, because you are about to be tipped back in the other direction on the see-saw of life. If you slip off, the karmic cycle starts over, and all those things you learned may have to be learned again. That sucks!

Know yourself. Know your limits on the way to becoming limitless. The more you learn about conscious knowing, the less likely you will get to the point of being at end of your rope, because you will have learned to find ways to allow, ask for, and find support where you perceived support wasn't there before. Just don't expect support from those who are not capable of offering it. Beg if you want to, but you might want hold those cards until you are really ready to play them on every level. Who is really testing you anyway; God or god? Remember that free will and intellect are not to be used only when it's convenient. Free will and intellect when used in the right way are used to help us claim our authentic power. Before we can become heart-centered, sometimes we need to call on our free will and our intellect to tell our heart that it is ok to open and raise the stakes.

When you are in this perceived end of your rope mode, and find yourself begging, go ahead and embrace the begging and saying "Please God". As you do this try changing the energy and meaning of the words "please God" from that of begging to the idea of *to please* and say "Please God". Change the energy again and say "Please god". Allow the begging please to be that of pleasure and change the capital "G" to a small "g" and see how that feels. You can simply begin to ask yourself what it would take to please the god in you. Keep repeating that to yourself until you FEEL the shift.

Sometimes we are so close and so immersed in a problem that we can't see beyond. Granted, some problems are simply bigger, harder to detach from and require more help. This is when you really need help processing the energy. Learn to know how to choose your battles and choose them wisely. Know when your patience has run out, but you won't win that poker pot if you throw the patience card too soon.

Maybe you don't really want answers. Maybe something inside you is afraid of the answer. Maybe you just aren't ready. Explore the fear. What's the absolute worst that could happen? Maybe in pondering that question and breaking it down over and over, you'll find that nothing is that big that it needs to be feared. There truth is there is no reason to fear yourself, because that's most likely what you will find.

Should you continue to ask the divine for answers? Yes, of course. Why? Because: praying is asking for help. Should you meditate? Yes. Why? Because: meditation is listening, and you can't really hear if you don't listen. Really, I mean meditate, not daydream and worry. Yes, you should meditate. I highly recommend it. You don't have to care about my opinion, just look at all the cultures that practice meditation and you can sense they are more peaceful.

Do you have to believe in God to ask and listen? Nope. Maybe not believing is part of the grand plan? So believer or not, don't judge it. If you say you don't believe because you just don't care anymore, that's apathy, not atheism. Play with the possibilities of believing and not believing. See where it leads you.

Being told that the answers are all within you doesn't mean that you have to go it alone. How many of us have an unconscious belief that we have to do everything ourselves? Telling someone all the answers are inside of them without a preface potentially compounds the problem of believing we are alone and have to do "it" all ourselves. That's not the intent of telling you that you already have all the answers.

A responsible coach/teacher/facilitator doesn't want to cripple you. They want guide you to a place where you can come up with your own answers. That doesn't mean you won't get pissed off in the process. We all need to be disturbed into seeking answers and creating change for the better. It doesn't mean you can't seek the help of others. Sometimes you will want to hide (The Hermit of the Tarot) and other times you will want to seek. Again, sometimes you just don't know what you just don't know, and you need help figuring it out. This can be a lesson in leaning to accept both being supported and to support self. Perhaps, you will begin to recognize that you are not alone or disconnected from pure source and that the feeling was a misperception to show you that you are connected.

You may need someone to just listen and/or be a sounding board. Often, in talking about something out loud, answers come; solutions are found. Do you know what a sounding board really is? It's a reflection of your voice. When you ask someone to be a sounding board are you implementing the tool correctly or are you just complaining? I'm not accusing here, just asking a question that you may want to ask yourself since complaining and blaming keeps you stuck in the past and prevents your from hearing what you need to hear, absorb and integrate.

It's a good idea to recognize being independent and interdependent. Slowing the idle chatter, being awake, aware and present will bring clarity to experiencing various ways of finding solutions. Going it alone is a great way to discover and embrace who you really are. Deep down we know everything is not black and white. Then again there are times we need to see things more black and white to eliminate confusion. Sounds contradictory and maddening, huh? This is precisely the time to call upon and trust our intuition and to ask your guides for intervention.

Give the solutions to your problems some breathing room. Breathing room will allow answers to come through. Give your experiences some breathing room, too. You just may become like fine wine. Just don't become a fine whiner or you could look like a wiener.

Focusing too hard on the problem or whining about it keeps you in that state of worry, stuck in the past and out of the present moment. Being in present moment does not mean that you should never plan for the future. Focusing only on the future keeps you in that constant state of wanting and desiring that keeps you out of present-moment awareness where your experiences are more profound.

Detaching is turning your problem over or surrendering to the will of the universe, but surrendering doesn't mean giving up. By detaching from the stress of not already having answers, God and all the divine beings who want to help, now have more freedom to intercede because you have let go, thereby stopping the tug-of-war that essentially you created by being too attached. If you need to grab the rope again as a lifeline, it will always be there to grab or gently tug when you need it. Hey, I need some help, please! Every time you grip onto something too tightly, put that picture of YOU holding onto God's leg like a child and see if you think it's flattering. That may be enough to stop you from being so needy.

Look at it from the divine's side. How do you function when someone doesn't give you the space you need to work? How does it feel when someone keeps begging and bugging to see if you are done yet? Get out of your own way. It's okay to ask for a progress report. That's accountability. If you don't learn this, you may end up with the self-imposed burden of disappointment.

Ask, turn it over, and then trust. Pay attention to the synchronicities that show up. Use discernment and find the answers you seek. Even when frustration makes you feel a bit maniacal when answers are revealed, it is magical.

While you are at it, please don't be the one who likes telling other people what to do. Are you the teller or the tellee? The "you shoulds" are irritating. None of us likes to be told what to do, so we need to do more teaching and less telling, more experience sharing and less "you shoulding", and more exploration of options, e.g., "you coulding". There is the exception when you see pointless harm or loss on the horizon. Then, yes, please tell. Nothing is black and white, well, except for pandas, zebras, penguins, orcas, parts of *Pleasantville*, the beginning of *The Wizard of Oz*…. Okay, okay, I'll stop. Oh, skunks and badgers. How could I forget them? (*Nirvana* –"Dumb" & "You Know You're Right")

Number Four Piss Me Off: Expectations.

When I was first told to lower my expectations, I took that as lowering my standards, which made me feel guilty. If my expectations are too high, I have a superiority complex. *Shit, I don't want to think or act like I am better than anyone else. I don't feel that way; I've never felt that way. I've attended the "Gathering of Equals." I am choosing equality. Am I really that horrible of a person? I'm so confused; don't you have to set higher standards to achieve your goals? I'm not worthy!* As I then slip into visions of Wayne and Garth I thought, *I wasn't meant to be a loser; this is b.s.* Again, the joke was on me.

Lowering your standards was presented to me by the same man who enlightened me to the concept of validation, creating a big "aha," so I believed him. I just misunderstood. When he told me that I had never been given validation for my feelings, my first thought was, *VALIDATION? You mean I am allowed to want validation? It's okay to want validation from people we love and care about? Really? I had no idea.* The thought of validation never entered my mind—other than for a parking pass—let alone to think I was worthy of expecting validation. Well, I didn't have it before, so why should I *expect* it now?

I did have aversion to the word "expectation," because I always heard my mother say, "You people expect me to 'insert anything' and don't show any appreciation." I never wanted to appear unappreciative, so telling me to lower my expectation when I didn't *think* I had expectation was a challenge for me to understand. How do I go less than zero?

On the other hand, if you have a need for constant validation, this is a major insecurity program. I suggest you find some techniques to assist you in overcoming your need and the fears associated with that need. You could try to observe where the insecurity and needy behavior began, and then embrace it, appreciate it, accept it, and say, "This no longer serves me. I have no reason to be insecure. I have no reason to doubt myself. I am well. I am good. I am whole."

It's not about lowering your standards. It's about lowering your expectation of others. They may not want what you want or be capable of understanding what you are beginning to understand presently. They are not where you are in the journey, so don't expect them to be.

This can be difficult in many areas of your life: work, employees, coworkers, friends, other personal interactions with doctors, cashiers, tellers (observe the analogies), on and on, especially family. I will never forget the day I was angry with my daughter because I had asked her to pick stuff up multiple times, and being one of those efficiency freaks—not so much control but efficiency—I was pissed. She may have been about ten. She said, "Mom, you're the only one who cares about the house being clean, so maybe you should be the one to do it."

Wow! Did that take me back to the lesson? My ego had no choice but to surrender. It was my expectation, not hers. It wasn't even really my expectation, but one that I was conditioned to as a child. Not everyone places the same importance on the same things. We all have our own priorities. So, I just said, "Yeah, you are right. But I do a lot of things for you that I don't care about, so maybe you could help me." She got "it" reluctantly, but she got it. And I got how much better it is to ask for cooperation than it is to expect.

How many of us as children and how many children still are served up some sort of punishment for speaking up like that when it is only an opportunity to communicate.

It's okay to have expectations, but they must be realistic. Create a sense of independence that you can be grateful for. Know what you can do on your own. Ask for help when needed. In doing so, you are taking responsibility for and supporting yourself. It doesn't mean you have to struggle. You will be at a much greater level of peace when you don't force your expectations on other people.

When you do something for someone else, and you feel disappointed or unappreciated, you may want to consider if whatever "it" is that you did was important to them or to you. If the "it" was important to you but not important to them, you may have set yourself up for disappointment, because you set the expectation. If you have been disappointed, does this help you embrace the idea of disappointment? Once you have, can you let it go?

In terms of creation, you are told that you get what you give. Giving is a wonderful blessing to all of us, both on the part of the giving and in the receiving. But I caution you: please don't be giving just because you *expect* something in return. That is giving from the ego and not from the heart center. It's not authentic, and, in a sense, it is actually manipulative. Please, whatever it is that you give, do it from your heart. Also, you don't have to give out of expectation to give. Choose from your heart when and what you want to give, and your giving and receiving will be more meaningful. When can you learn to just say no? When can you be more generous? When can you be more accepting of generosity and simply say, *thank you*?

It's a law of nature to expect results from your efforts. Just remember that things don't always work out the way you expect them to, and you and your efforts may be rewarded from a different source. Be responsible for your own actions. Remain in integrity. Remember that in the kindness of giving, you may receive in ways you never expect and will be more appreciative of what you receive.

When it comes to manifesting the life you desire, we all develop in different ways and speeds, because we all have had different expectations and experiences. This is an aspect of awareness where we can begin to let go of judgment. Some of us are or have been damaged, and we need time to repair some of that damage before we can move along.

Did I say move along? Next up, *The All American Rejects* with "Move Along." Sometimes all these creative artists make me feel like I am the reject. Nah, that's not it. Many artists are really good at channeling and expressing the dysfunction they experienced.

One more thought on expectations before we move along: if we are all creators, and we all have free will to create heaven on earth, then maybe we should not expect God to fix things any more than we should expect our parents to fix things or try to fix our kids or anyone else for that matter.

Chapter 4

More Misinterpretations; Confusing Letting Go with Denial

Part A. Confusing Letting Go with Denial

This is one that happens more often than we can admit. Really? Did I just say that about denial?

Many, in their attempt to let go, actually take a problem and bury it, push it down, deny it. This is a big red flag, which can create all kinds of problems and chaos, including illness. It's the proverbial Band-Aid. When you push anything down, where do you think it goes? It goes as far as you want it to. It can go all the way to the *bowels* of hell, where you create your own personal hell, which is a big miscreation. It can also become the proverbial wall around the castle which blocks our dreams or can outright stop us from becoming who we are truly intended to be.

Many of us deny being in denial. Is it really worth putting yourself through hell? Seems to me there is a connection somewhere between denial and salvation that we have heard but not absorbed. How many times have you said or heard someone say that it felt good to get something off their chest? Stop for a second. Right now, remember a time when you got something off your chest and it felt really good.

Did it make you feel lighter? Did it feel like a burden was lifted? Did it feel honest? Did it feel rare and real? It's the feeling that a weight has been lifted. Could there have been so much weight that the pressure expanded beyond the heart to the chest or farther? Hmm...could added weight be a protection mechanism? What about the excessive weight someone losses when they have cancer? Could that be something eating away at them?

Regardless of how someone responds to your truth, can you feel better about yourself? Even if you feel sad for the other person's inability to accept the truth, do you feel better about expressing truth and honesty? In dark times, can you feel your *Dark Knight Rising* or allow you inner Superman to bring about truth and justice within you? Have you seen times when you have brought forth truth and justice that it opens the door for others to do the same? Are you willing to stay out of your ego and accept those times when others are not ready, willing, or able to tap into their inner superhero?

Too often letting go is an excuse for ignoring. Trust me, more often than not, ignoring is not the solution. Ignoring and forgetting only have value when there is no one else who will benefit from the knowing.

If you had a physical wound, most likely you would give it some attention or treatment so it could heal properly. Why don't we treat our emotional wounds with the same care? Many of us have been taught to bury our feelings because when we sought help, the people that we sought help from, had no knowledge of how to appropriately handle the wound so their ego responded rather than the authentic self. Fear can be a lack of knowledge or information. With fear comes false emotion including embarrassment. Along with that is a fear of confrontation. Rather than lose the fear, seek the knowledge and confront the situation head on the shame and embarrassment is passed on to the seeker. Can you see now how physical ailments try to get our emotional attention?

So which is it? Have you really let go? Are you in the process of letting go? Or are you denying? Is something so painful that you can only allow whatever "it" is to come up a little at a time? If so, that's okay because that can be part of the process of letting go. You determine how fast or slow you will go, and sometimes you need a break from yourself to experience some enjoyment. It's those moments of enjoyment that will make you more determined to butter yourself up and allow betterment in. After all, everything is better with butter...oh, and bacon and cheese.

If you are burying or denying something because you think you are protecting someone else, that may work for a while, but it's dishonest. Can we really not handle the truth? I'll bet you are stronger than you think you are. In fact, I would venture to say your strength is limitless. My honesty tells me that we don't give kids enough credit when we think they are too young to handle the truth. Often children handle the truth better than those in adult bodies. Sure, a game of charades is fun for a while when it's something light, but...can you recall a time when you found out something heavy that was hidden from you with the idea that it was for your own protection? What's the typical reaction to that? Anger? So why, why, why would you continue to hide something from yourself when every part of your being is shaking you and screaming for your attention, ready to find a way to let go? For me, I actually had a dream that I was dead, and I met someone important to me who said, "You let me live a lie." With that dream, I chose a path of truth and wisdom.

This is to get you thinking and feeling. Denial is a topic that could be a book in itself. Trust me, as a child, I denied things, thinking I was protecting people around me, because denial is a behavior I was conditioned to since birth and probably in other lifetimes. Trust me when I say that denial only perpetuates dysfunctional behavior that is so prevalent in this world. We need to be taught that when something is wrong with the picture, the picture needs a deeper look and it shouldn't be covered up by photoshopping it. We don't need x-rays or x-ray vision to take a "fantastic voyage."

Denial is dishonest. Denial is a choice. Which one feels better to you? Very seriously, no excuses, no ifs, no ands, no buts, no justifying, no left or right brain allowed, one direct question here "shot through the heart" (yes, we found a *Bon Jovi* song), which feels better, honest or dishonesty?

Struggling to get out of your head with that question or not, let's listen to *Bon Jovi's* "You Give Love a Bad Name." But when you listen, use it as a metaphor and see if you are using blame as an excuse to not let go, because there is no blame, just human experience.

There is talk about spiritual contacts but, really, what does that mean? Well, that's an agreement we made before we incarnated. It's a soul contract. So here is an example of denial: if I have a spiritual contract with a person to show me a lesson, convincing myself that I can just accept that something happened and dismiss the happening because of a contract is the same as saying, "That's just how it is" or "That's the way things are" or "It's my karma," when sometimes "just how it is" is not okay. That is still denial, not letting go. And, yes, I have heard someone excuse staying in an abusive relationship, because they say they have a contract.

If you are aware enough to know that a contract exists, then be responsible enough to do something about it. There could be fear or underlying fear stopping you from taking some form of action, so you dismiss the contract by saying that you are accepting your karma. Yeah, that works. Hold on to that karma. We wouldn't want to break a dysfunctional cycle, would we? Yes, that was sarcasm. If you are using karma as an excuse, then you are denying your free will. You do have a choice to either fulfill or break it.

To really break free, there has to be some sort of conclusion. Some refer to this as cutting cords. There are circumstances where it may be preferable to not just cut the cords but to remove them altogether. We can distance ourselves physically from a situation, but we also want to do this emotionally and energetically by removing the emotional trauma from our bodies where we hold it. Removing it from our body not only reduces the risk of illness but makes your life feel lighter, alive, and free. Until you know how to do this, and even after, this is something you will need help with from an energy practitioner. Get your ego out of the way and stop resisting help by saying, "I can do this myself." Resistance likes to walk hand in hand with denial. Let those two go off on their own and hold onto the idea of "misery loves company." They've got each other (more *Bon Jovi,* "Livin' on a Prayer"). The process works much better when you are supported. Convincing yourself you are fine does not reach a conclusion.

There are those who say, "Oh, I don't understand all that contract stuff, and I don't want to. Guess what. That's denial, too. This is why "breaking up is hard to do." Sorry, that song is too old for me to listen to it. It was written in the day when there was too much black and white in, oh, so many ways. The black and white of that time is a metaphor that runs way too deep into judgment, which we would all like to forget, but guess what. Not forgetting still serves to help others break free and step into a world of color. Please, stop making excuses, especially for denial.

Be wary when you hear yourself or someone say, "I'm fine." What level of fine are we talking about? Are you at complete peace or just coping? Are you fine or are you good? Again, there are some things better off buried and forgotten, but that is only when they are no longer important. If the burial and forgetting is a setup— which creates a deep-rooted issue in the form of repression or suppression to whatever degree—that action will not bring you to any type of resolve. Burial without grief resolution doesn't work regardless if it is an issue or physical death. If you leave the gas on without a flame, you will have an explosion. That's what happened to me around thirty.

Sometimes "fine" and "okay" are dangerous words. There is the power of the positive convincing us that everything is fine. It's not that things can't be fine, but sometimes things aren't fine. Sure, there are those who over-dramatize and think the sky is falling when it isn't, but that's the opposite extreme and not what we are talking about here on the topic of denial. The power of the positive leads us to believe that unless we convince ourselves that we are fine or that we will be fine, we will be or appear to be negative. The danger in convincing ourselves that we are fine lies below the surface where an unattended wound can fester. Allowing it to fester is essentially being less than honest, honorable, nurturing, or self-supportive. What we perceived as being positive and strong can actually backfire and create a backdraft. Transmuting anger and expressing honesty are what makes the power of the positive more than just lip service and fans the flame of passion and compassion.

It's no wonder that when we hear the concept of contracts—and that we chose the lesson before we came here—we go to the space of guilt, shame, blame, and embarrassment. You tell yourself that you asked for it, or "It's my karma." We were setup to misinterpret. How many times were we told as a child, "You asked for it," and it wasn't true? The vibration of the way that "you asked for it" is expressed to us as children changes the vibration of being able to accept that in another realm we actually in some way did.

While most adults are simply not aware of the potential repercussions of their words, that doesn't excuse their poor choice of those words. An adult body does not a grown-up make. As adults, we may be intellectually capable to accept that sticks and stones don't break our bones, but we still have it unconsciously stored in our memory banks. Sometimes it would be nice to have the capacity to delete cookies and files, but if we did, there would be that danger of looking for the instant fix, like in the *Eternal Sunshine of the Spotless Mind*.

Our memories have value, and we can use them to help ourselves and help others in a positive way. While the right words might be used in saying that "we asked for it," because we did make an agreement in another realm, they have been expressed in the wrong way, which has imprinted a whole new meaning on our psyche. It's likely that the people who are saying, "You asked for it," aren't conscious enough to know that the idea of divine contract exists. In that case, knowingly or unknowingly, even their intention isn't nurturing. Wake up and pay attention to how you use your words.

All this crap, contradiction, and lack of understanding make it difficult for us to let go. It keeps us in denial of being responsible for creating our lives. The guilt and the shame are in opposition to being responsible and accountable, which is really the way it should be. No wonder people in this world have difficulty with personal responsibility; they are clueless to the meaning. Our job is to try to untangle the wiring in our brain of whatever we set up. Okay, song time. *Carly Simon,* "Heard It Should Be." From now on, question "how it should be?"

Particularly with abuses, there is so much denial and there are so many kinds of abuse: sex, drug and alcohol, substance, verbal, emotional, physical, domestic, financial. It's all abuse of power and denial comes into play on the part of both—the abuser and the abused. Then there is neglect. All are affected. It's nearly unfathomable to think that abuse of some sort hasn't affected every single one of us on this planet on some level. Someone should write a song about "excuse for abuse."

When someone has been raised in an abusive situation, they often don't know any other way, so there is no reference to know that they are being abused. Nor do they recognize that they have been or are being subjected to more than one kind. One might not know any other way, completely unaware and actually take comfort in the abuse because it is familiar. We are creatures of habit, and we become comfortable with what we know and uncomfortable with what we don't know.

Then comes more excuses when someone is injured in some way: "Oh, they didn't mean it." Not meaning it doesn't excuse it. Abuse is not kind. Abuse is not compassionate; it's not conscious.

Abuse is not acceptable and has no value in our world if our goal is to achieve inner and outer peace, freedom, and joy.

We should remember that abused and abusers both need help. Why do people abuse, and why does the abused so often become an abuser? Is it a way to justify their actions or to make what happened to them seem okay? Is it an ego-based response of protection? Ideally, knowing the ego would help in correcting abusive behavior. With so many types of abuses, it's common to transform into another type or multiple types of abuser. The abuse is either turned inward or outward, and either way, it's an "excuse" or a way to "excuse"—same word, same spelling, just a different pronunciation.

Attracting more abuse may be your soul's way of showing you the dysfunctional cycle you have been caught in and expose that it is unacceptable. Are you ready to accept that there was value in the lesson, but abuse is not ok? Are you ready to accept yourself and move into an internal and external environment that is nurturing and supportive?

When you step into your own divinity and/or authenticity, remaining denial starts to make you feel guilty, because it knows you aren't honoring yourself. When you begin to honor yourself, you can begin to honor the pain, embrace it until it gives up, and let it go.

Knowing you are not honoring yourself becomes disturbing. The Indian mystic Osho said, "I love to disturb people, because only by disturbing them can I make them think." He also said, "I am not going to console anybody." He believed that our challenges would bring us to a climax. We have to feel disturbed to be motivated to make change. If that starts with thinking, because you aren't ready to feel from your heart, and you aren't ready to tear down the fortress, at least you are thinking about it, pondering it, imagining it. It's a start.

As long as we live in a world full of pain, "just how it is" is not acceptable. This from *Alice in Chains*—"Down in a Hole."

"Down in a hole, feelin' so small
Down in a hole, losin' my soul
I'd like to fly,
But my wings have been so denied."

Stop denying your wings. Feel the winds of change. Allow yourself to feel your wings. Let the wind lift you up, and let not only your heart soar but your entire being. As in the song "Mornin", know that you are worthy to reach out your hand and touch the face of God.

Part B. Denial of a Different Form

There is another form of belief around denial. There is a belief that to be enlightened, we must let go of all our earthly wants, desires and cravings; that we must deny ourselves (deny *yourself*?). Here again is something that has been taken too literal. While giving up anything for a period of a time has value, such as TV, sugar, chemical-laden food, and, particularly, idle chatter in the brain, there remains that possibility that giving up everything permanently has the opposite extreme and does allow fulfillment of the authentic self. Where is enjoyment in this belief? It's difficult to have a flame of passion when the pilot isn't lit. Shouldn't you – "Let Your Soul Be Your Pilot" – *Sting*. How can you have joy without the action of participating in something that creates joy?

While this form of denial can lead to the emptiness required so that we can refill the kettle and start cooking with passion, living only an inward journey without participating in an outward journey can leave you feeling just as hollow as an outward journey without an inward journey. Going to temple on Saturday, going to church on Sunday, or going to any other service without really digesting the good or not being able to digest what you are being force fed is going through motions without fulfillment. Our lessons must be both palatable and digestible. If not, you need to find another place to eat, eat at home, or go on a liquid fast for a while, both physically and metaphorically. Keep in mind there is a key in the word "service" as, often, those who are the most fulfilled live in some type of service to others.

If you crave something, then taste it, as long as you aren't sucking someone else's blood physically, energetically, or otherwise. If your cravings tend towards causing yourself or other people pain, you need to deny yourself and seek professional help. Having some Hungarian lineage, I've encountered that feeling of having the life blood sucked right out of me.

Much of the problem we face starts when we allow marketing to manipulate us into *thinking* we need something outside of us to bring us satisfaction, and we are obsessed by not denying ourselves anything. This is fairly obvious in the outside world; we've got that concept intellectually under control even though we still *buy* into trappings. Those who are on an inward journey succumb to buying crystals, oil, incense, and more. Me, too! They are beautiful, they smell beautiful, and they are powerful tools, but they are still just the tool. It's our job to implement the tool.

Often we crave things we "think" we want but are left unsatisfied or bored when we get those things. Then we are left wanting more or something else. We end up accumulating a bunch of crap, and the shit piles get deep. We feel disappointment. This is the time to look inward. We should be using the crap as compost and turn it into fertilizer.

By not cultivating the inside and the outside of self, we can create the false feelings of unworthiness or entitlement to the extreme. We start to deny ourselves based on unworthiness and fear of disappointment, and we tend to take on the *expectation* of wanting someone or something else to fix or fulfill us. If you need a Band-Aid (the aid of a band, music and sound) then use it.

Sound and vibration help break up stuck patterns and vicious circles, especially the vibration of words from the past that haunt us. We have to be open to listening; recognizing that we have options and choosing the sounds that create harmony for us.

Those who don't feel they have support but have a strong will (solar plexus chakra), will want to seek support from reliable sources and not expect support from those who are incapable of offering it. *Ayah Asher Ayah (explanation to follow in the chapter on intentions).*

The concept of "you have to want *it* for yourself" and "find your own answers" contains the element of personal responsibility, which lowers your expectations. Help is there if you want it, but you have to crave it *for* yourself. It's not about letting go of craving but tapping into what your soul craves. How about craving peace? Can you feel that?

Taking an outward journey without taking an inward journey defies the laws of our nature. It is in embracing both the inner and outer that turns our natural world into the supernatural that knows no fear.

Now that was a deeper level. So if you really are just craving a piece of chocolate, go ahead, for God's sake, have a piece of chocolate. Just let it be. Allow some things to be a pointless pleasure; laugh and play with purpose and without. Seriously, did I say, "Let It Be"? Okay, then, *The Beatles,* just not fried or chocolate-covered. EW.

Chapter 5

To Tell The Stories, or Not To Tell The Stories?

Yeah, yeah, yeah, we all have stories, right? Yes, that was a bad *Beatles* pun since they were the last up on the playlist.

Yes, I know, I talk about my stories in this book, but trying to tell the story third party feels dishonest. So it is what it is.

You will often hear a coach say, "Stay out of the story." Not getting stuck in the story doesn't mean that the facts of the story don't have merit, or that you can't hit the highlights of the story to help the facilitator have some knowledge, empathy, or compassion to work with and bestow you with wisdom or insight in solving your problem. Whew!

Let your internal will help you stick to the facts. Your story isn't wrong. *You may be wrong but, you may be right.* Did you hear *Billy Joel* there, too? Listen to yourself from your observer's perspective. Check with your integrated self to be sure it's not some fear-based idea of what you might sound like. Can you listen without considering what someone else's idea would be of what you *should* say? Can you consider what you feel like without feeling bad about how you really feel? Honor and embrace how you feel. Identifying is part of the process.

Finally choosing to lick and heal my wounds, I was still playing the victim of sound bites from pre and post-wounding. I believed it was burdensome on someone else, even a counselor, to tell my story, so I believed the story "should" remain untold. Quite a challenge it was to tell the story without the story. It required a lot of overthinking and was quite exhausting. No wonder I have headaches. I would dance around the story from the perspective of already having the solution, just to see if I was "thinking" clearly and if my feelings were "valid." *But then if all the answers were inside of me, and if I am not supposed to doubt what my heart said, then I should be good and not have to tell anyone anything. Shit. I'm already supposed to be fixed, but I feel so bad. How can I go on pretending? What's wrong with me? I know I need help, but how am I supposed to get it without asking and telling my story? What if my honesty makes someone else mad? I can't tell my story because no one needs to validate me but me, and my dad said all I need is a good crack in the ass. Ugh! Really! How is this helping me!* If I told any part of my story, I felt like such a whiner. I don't recall being constipated, but I needed a good shit fit. I also recall being told as a kid, "You have no business telling anyone else your business." Yeah, ok. That made a lot of sense. Not!

We all know it's not a good idea to get stuck in the ego side of "he said," "she said," and then "they said" or the overly emotional side of "I said." We can try not to point fingers, but unless you know how to express, it takes practice not to do that. Often we come out looking like the bad guy, because other parties are listening with their ego. So everybody's egos get in the way. Integrity shows us the bad guy, the not so bad guy and the veritable good guy within so that we can make improvements regardless of how others react as we learn how to express appropriately.

Telling the same old worn-out story over and over is what keeps you stuck in the past, unless you are exercising perseverance and looking for clues that you may have missed. Thing is, that won't happen, unless you take a break from beating yourself up and allow awareness to take over. Not telling your story is really about sticking to the facts and getting down to the heart of the issue, not the mundane details of the story. Sometimes the tiniest details creates the "aha" moment. If some small detail seems to keep jumping up and down, saying, "Look at me," give it some attention. Ask the detail what it wants to tell you. It may be an important fact.

Not only listen to, but hear your story, and allow aspects to show up that will provide clarity to change the energetic charge on the story so you can...let it go...and move beyond. Omitting facts that are important can be a form of self-sabotage. We are human. Embrace the emotion, the anger, the pain, so you can understand it. An embrace is not a place where you can stay; it must be broken. That doesn't mean you can't have another. Getting stuck in a story loop is a sure way to drive you insane.

Chaos is created when you stay in a state of being overly emotional or under-emotional (numb). Embrace what you are feeling completely so you can let go completely, but then give the embrace of the emotion some time to settle down. You do not operate like a light switch, so don't expect yourself to.

The new agers like to tell you to just send love to whatever is bothering you. While that may be an altruistic idea, it isn't always realistic, particularly if you have experienced trauma. Some are protecting their heart and therefore, it's just not that simple to wish something away with love. Some need to reach a level of acceptance before they can begin to feel love. With so much emotional trauma in our world, it's no wonder why so many perceive new age as hocus pocus or airy-fairy even if the best intentions are at play. If you are not over "it" yet, there likely are other aspects that you need to look at, and it may require peeling those layers back one at a time, until you get to the root cause or core.

There was a point where I really resonated by peeling back the layers. Because there is no one right or wrong way, sometimes you want to dig down to the roots and pluck the weed. Other times, you want to remove the outer layers as they are ready to be released. The issue may be so deep that you have to journey to the center of the earth to find that core.

But we really don't eat the core of anything. Taking nourishment from whatever we are eating to get to the core is one thing, but the core is not what feeds or sustains us.

Getting to the core can be the ultimate point where you discover, and are able to release, what wants to be released. There is a place inside of the core where seeds of new life lie and from where our true passion begins to erupt. It is an ending point and a new beginning.

Within the metaphor of peeling back layers and getting to the core, you see that you have a choice to toss that core away or toss it into fertile soil. As joy returns and you feel new life in your steps, you just might find you get what you need (*Rolling Stones'*—"Can't Always Get What You Want"). Then, again, sometimes we find that what we needed is better than what we wanted. As you resonate more with the other side of the spectrum, the idea of the flower blossom opening one petal at a time until the full bloom is presented with all its magical beauty becomes more appealing. Remember there was beauty in each step of the blossoming process. Your garden feels more like home. The fragrance brings euphoric joy, and we can drink in the sweetness of the nectar. On the earth, the flower would not be there to blossom without the turmoil at the core and the subsequent volcanic eruption to create the ground, where new growth can begin and ultimately the blossoming occurs. I didn't always see this, let alone feel it.

There was a time when I felt jealousy towards those who had achieved this peace. I pray that if you are searching for peace, you will continue on your journey until you find it. I dove into the belly of the beast to get there, but you don't always have to do it the hard way. Now that I know that Jonah's whale was just an underwater spacecraft—thanks to the Tsoukalicious folks at *Ancient Aliens*—it makes everything much easier knowing that we can be released from the beast and not digested by it.

Depending on where you are emotionally, imagine a flower of your choice in your heart. Breathe. Transform it from a flat 2-D picture to 3-D, and then make it panoramic. Now, feel it all around you 360 degrees in every direction. Breathe it into your heart. Breathe that into your body. Allow it to show you beauty. Send it out. Bring it back in and keep the feeling for yourself as we continue.

"Hey, guys, with all your colors dancing around having fun, Martha here. I hear the laughter and the joy. It's awe-inspiring, awesum and AWE FULL. I am grateful and all, but I am still operating in linear earth time. We have a little more, so we need to move on. What's that? You are reminding me that there is KNOW TIME where things happen in divine time? Yes, I remember. Isn't that why we took that little party break? Yes. Oh, you wanted me to point that out to the readers, okay."

One more deep breath and out with a little sound.

Depending on what you have been through, you can't necessarily feel love for yourself until you reach this point. When you get to the core, the story isn't so important. If you have experienced abuse or trauma, the idea of self-love can be difficult. Self-love is something that I definitely choked on, yes'd, and whatever'd for a long time. My first therapy encounter was with a counselor who went all Al Franken/Stuart Smalley, look in the mirror, and say "I love you" crap on me...really? Funny on TV, not in my reality. I could have thrown in the towel right then. A good therapist will spot that is not the right place to start. If you find yourself in this situation, don't allow it to discourage you from seeking answers.

At the time, love was not the "Shape of My Heart" (*Sting*). Seeing so much anger, frustration, and hatred in the world, I would imagine many would benefit from heart reshaping.

Not that I couldn't talk about love at all, but I was challenged to express it freely with people. The idea of love, being loved, and being lovable seemed impossible. The word "love" was not used often in my house. If you showed it, you were certain to be squashed in some way. I remember saying it to my dad once, and he couldn't say it back. I now recognize the pain in his eyes as he pursed his lips, unable to respond. At the time, a part of me recognized and accepted his inability, but my ego was more in control, so it caused slight damage compounded by my mother blaming him for her inability to express.

It's all good now. We can try to intellectualize this as adults, but the pain cannot be erased until we learn to accept and forgive. At the risk of defending what I am saying, I will say that I know there are many of us out there who have experienced the same thing or similar. This made even more obvious to me when I went through my Oneness Deeksha Giver training. There was not one person in that room who didn't have the desire to have love expressed to them more freely by their parents. Many of the World War II generation had a difficult time with expressing at all, let alone expressing love. They responded in a way they were conditioned to respond. It was a different time for them and a different time now for us. We've chosen differently. We see differently, so it's our responsibility to change how we interact with the world around us and begin to express not only love but unconditional love that does not come with the expectation of love.

So there was a slight bit of damage in me, because my parents didn't say "I love you." Oh, boo hoo – Big deal, right? We are supposed to just know that we are loved, right? What about when trauma completely removes being lovable from your reality? Wondering what it would have been like if things were different serves no purpose to us, but it shows us a new way to make something better for someone else.

For me, being lovable was removed from reality because I was sexually abused not just by one person who I was supposed to be able to trust, but by two. Not only were these two, men who I was supposed to be able to trust, but by conventional definition they were men who should have loved and cared about me. As a child, this creates a great deal of confusion. As a kid, you don't really give a whole lot of consideration to the idea of being lovable, but we are taught only bad people get punished, and sexual abuse feels like punishment. There were many reasons that I kept quiet, but one was that I was terrified of being perceived as a bad person. Bad = Unlovable. This belief is imposed upon us from many sources.

As I was coming up with how to express this for the book, I was reminded by a cough. In the past, exploring memory would have knocked me out of present moment and sent me on a downward spiral. This time, I was simply reminded how I used to choke on the idea of being lovable when the idea of such was brought into my awareness. One way we express is through our voice, so choking expressed not only my inability to express freely but also how it made me sick to believe I could never be loved. Further it reminded that being unlovable was not caused by anyone or anything, rather it was an experience I chose to give me the opportunity to express how free will can create change and give a voice to others.

Luckily participating in workshops, with facilitators who understand the importance of not pushing someone past where they are ready to go has made it easier for me to heal and incorporate that same premise into my own energy practice. It is of great importance to allow someone's heart to open when the soul is ready, so we can eventually realize that everything *is* about love.

It's okay to disturb someone or be disturbed to the point of readiness, but they must choose the step. Pushing too hard, too fast can open an emotional wound that could hinder healing. We can offer possibilities that inspire courage but it is not our place to force.

I have discovered that embracing all that has happened to us along with deliberate breath not only helps us let go but also reveals the value of what happened. That doesn't mean what happened was okay.

In learning to accept self-love, it is often easier to feel love for others than to feel love for one's self. Sending love out with the in breath and then returning to the self with the out breath opens a doorway to allow one to feel love for self. Go ahead and give it a try. Try using your hands to guide you. Start with your hands together. As you breathe in, open your arms and send out love. Then, on the out breath, return your hands together at your heart. Observe how that feels. Do you feel the crack to allow love in?

You've emptied yourself on the out breath ready to be filled.

Now, open your arms, ready to receive. On the in breath, allow love to flow to you as you bring your hands together and cross your arms at your heart. Feel the release as you breathe out and open your arms again. Observe that feeling.

It takes a little practice, but the practice of sending and receiving opens the door for you to get what you give, and the giving and receiving of love is one of the greatest gifts we have in our human experience. Once you break that ice, then you can allow love to move through you.

We must learn to know and sense love from a place of being fully present before we can really begin to consider feeling unconditional love, which will heal the planet. If you are having difficulty with love, you can begin by working with your solar plexus chakra. This is your power center, your strength, courage, and will. Once you muster up strength from there, without the ego in the way, you can see that strength and courage are elements of vulnerability eventually leading to your heart. Another technique that I like is to send all the crap down to the molten core of the earth, and let Mother Earth transmute fear and pain and bring it back into your body fresh and vital. If you feel the energy moving in another pattern, allow it. Follow it and see where it leads you.

As you allow yourself to begin to resonate with the idea of love, you will automatically find expressing from the heart more comfortable, along with being kinder and more compassionate.

Once you begin to feel love, you may enjoy creating a garden in your home vessel (your physical body). You can pluck out that which has no value from the root and dispose of it into the compost pile where your past memories become the fertilizer of true awakening. Disposing of the past allows us to be present and to step into the creative state. Disposing of the past allows us to be an empty vessel that is ready to be filled again. Reaching this state is very powerful, and the idea of living fulfilled is ignited with passion.

The fact is that we, as humans, like stories. We relate to stories. We learn from stories. We love to listen to stories. We bond together on stories. So stories do have great value. Our stories spark emotion, empathy, and compassion. But...pay attention to what your story sounds like. If you can't stand listening to yourself anymore, change it. Turn what once appeared maniacal to something magical. Stories can offer the ability to transform emotion and create the "aha" that we seek as you say yes to being the seeker.

When we wrong our emotions, we suppress them. That's when the internal conflict turns into a revolution. It's an attempt to fight back, but war is not the way to peace. You are entitled to your human emotions. You are entitled to stand up for yourself. Being stuck in emotion from past trauma can become self-destructive. Being in any emotional state, heightened or numb, creates a feeling of being immobilized. We are not robots. *"Are we human or are we dancers?"* Only a fan of *The Killers* would get that reference. I feel a break coming. Read the lyrics; listen to the song.

Just remember to appreciate that while there may be periods when pain causes us to be immobile. The immobility may be there to help us face the story. There comes a point when emotional pain can move us into action, or even make us want to dance. We all have a different tolerance level for pain. Can you choose to use your emotions to set you free and dance? Why keep reliving the pain? As the song says, "Cut the cord," I say, "Cut the cord to your story and dance."

Chapter 6

Three Silly Questions

I need a break from the intensity of this book. How about you? So I have a few questions that maybe you can answer for me. Every time I ever asked these questions, I get a blank stare.

1. Why is "oh, my God" considered by some a curse? When I say it, there are only two possible meanings. Number one, I am saying a prayer for strength and patience. I am really saying, "Oh, my God, give me strength and patience to deal with this stupidity." Number two, if something exciting has happened, I could be saying thank you. "Oh, my God, how wonderful! Thank you." The "thank you" is recognition of the godliness in the person offering the wonder that has made me full. So how is "oh, my God" taking God's name in vain? I just don't get it. Which brings up this point: it's not the words themselves but the intent of the words that create the vibration. I must have heard that somewhere.

2. Why do we have duality in third dimension? Does that mean there is triality in fourth dimension or quadrality in the fifth? Really, I've asked that question before, and I usually get a blank look, and the subject changes. Even *Carl Sagan* said of fourth dimension; "We can't imagine it".

3. If "grateful" means full of gratitude and "wonderful" is full of wonder, then why does "awful" typically denote something

horrible instead of full of awe? Isn't "awesome" only somewhat in awe? "Oh, it's awesome! Yes, I am in awe but only some." Does that mean "awesome" is a celebration of mediocrity? This usually gets blank stares, too. I think "awful" has gotten a bad rap. Since it is unlikely we will dispense with saying awesome, shouldn't we at least change the spelling to awesum, which would be the sum of awe? Who provoked that thought, was that you Emma?

On to a song that is not really as silly as it may sound *Crash Test Dummies* – "Mmm Mmm Mmm Mmm".

Chapter 7

Intention Creates Intervention, but Intention Alone Is Not Enough

B efore you start this chapter, please take a deep breath. Breathe the idea and the feeling of love into your heart, and then breathe it out. When you do this, be aware of your heart. Breathe in as deeply as you can; hold it for a second or two, then let it out. How often do we catch ourselves holding our breath when something is stressful? So now, this time, think about peace and love flowing in you and through you. Hold the breath momentarily and release. As you see it, also allow yourself to feel it. As you practice expanding your awareness, see, feel, and notice that love is all around you, 360 degrees in every direction. Add more dimension if you can. Just don't hold your breath so long that you pass out. That would be silly.

No matter what you do in life, develop and maintain integrity to help with your integration. Often we confuse a belief with integrity. This is where we get into trouble, because a belief can become rigid and may interfere with flexibility, preventing you from "bending like a reed in the wind." There is a difference between believing in yourself, believing you can achieve something, and imposing a belief. Learn to know the difference. Ask yourself questions. Is something really true, or am I just holding onto a rigid belief? You may *think* you know the answer right away, or maybe you *think* you don't know the answer. Watch out if there is a little too much conviction in your answer; that could be a clue. If you think there are no possibilities other than what you *think*, be prepared for a lesson.

Ask yourself; *am I holding on to a belief out of fear? Holding on because I never considered another possibility? Is it possible that there are other possibilities?* How about this one, have you ever said to yourself, *there is no other possible way*? Do you know someone who thinks like this? Recognize that a fear is not necessarily something you have a direct fear of, like spiders or snakes. In other words, it's not necessarily the thing that you have a fear of but something under the surface within us that causes you to rigidly hold on. One possibility is the fear of not being accepted. You could be holding on to a belief, because you fear losing face with an individual or a group. Do you recognize this fear in yourself right now or in the past? Are you willing to risk not being your authentic self? Or are you now willing to speak up and speak the truth?

Having a fear created by a belief of something we were taught or led to believe without considering the truth is prevalent. This is conditioning, whether intentional or unintentional and has been going on throughout history. These conditioned beliefs are out of our awareness. The level of unawareness comes from the depth of the conditioning. So, in accepting that we are multidimensional beings, consider that awareness is a factor in setting intentions from a standpoint of integrity. Without awareness, you may be setting intentions that have an aspect of conditioning and in turn setting yourself up for self-sabotage. To live authentically, you must breakdown the conditioning and conformity. Ask: *Is this really my intent? Or is it someone else's idea of a good intent? Is it another "should"? This desire that I have—is it mine or was it imposed upon me? Does my authentic- self desire this? Will it bring me fulfillment?*

Though you will hear me say that lack is a conditioned belief within our societies across the planet, it's pretty obvious that I believe there is a lack of integrity within our human moral fiber. I am not saying that moral fiber doesn't exist; I am saying that we need to do a much better job. On the other hand, there are a lot of people doing a fantastic job.

It appears this chapter is more about integrity and awareness than it is about intentions. No, not really. It was just a preface, so that you can be really clear about your desires before you set your intentions in stone. Hmmm...set it in stone. Watch that, too. You will want to be as *clear and present* as possible before you set your intents; otherwise, you might encounter some *danger*. Unless, of course, it is your intent to change your name to *Austin* and it is danger that you seek. Go for it, but I don't think that's what most of us are looking for. Maybe a little adrenaline rush now and then, but not real danger, unless *Danger* is your middle name.

By now, you can see the benefit in having integrity and awareness present in setting intentions. Without these elements, we may set intentions that aren't necessarily heart-centered or coming from a place of our purpose or passion. Be flexible with your intentions and stay out of expectations. For example, we all want more money, right? There is always something we want more of. We are conditioned by stimuli around us to want more and conditioned to believe we are lacking in general. Not that there is anything wrong with wanting more, and it's okay to have wants for yourself, but I would suggest that you question your integrity and awareness as to why you need more. It's okay to have something solely for pleasure but be cautious of greed. Is your intent selfish or selfless? Self-indulgence is good for us once and a while. How will getting what you want change your life? How will it change others' lives? Will this intention allow me to live my fulfilled?

In our current reality, we need money. We took the reality of not needing money away from the Native Americans because of a rigid belief of who was right and who was wrong. Uh-oh, I must resist going off on a tangent. Breathe, breathe. Okay...I am good. So, it would be fantastic if we didn't need money, but we haven't evolved past that just yet. Be clear on why you want money. If the only intent to have money is to have money for money's sake so you can sit on your ass and be taken care of, then be careful, because karma might take your ass away from you. A good idea is to let go of the idea of lack. After all, our purpose here is to master third dimension and break the dysfunctional karmic cycles, so why create one?

If you try to play off that wanting material possessions is for your children, then you are teaching them to buy into the same societal norms that we bought into, which have created the mess we are in today. A really good example of an imposed societal belief and conditioning would be the story of *The Lottery* by Shirley Jackson and the five monkeys experiment. In the story of *The Lottery*, each year, a person was sacrificed and no one even remembered why. In the five monkeys experiment, it was a matter of conditioning and societal beating with no rationality. Unfortunately, things like this still exist today and are done from a premise of ritual, conditioning, and belief with no considerations of why, common decency, or common sense. If you are going to be angry about anything, why not get angry about things that are less than humane? How about setting an intention on effecting change that starts inside each of us? What actions could you take now for that to happen?

While it may be altruistic and too big for one person to set his or her intent to live in a society like the idea of Camelot, it's an intent that could change things for future generations that just might include us, if we believe we live more than one life. Just because passive and creative societies of the past were destroyed by the more aggressive societies, it doesn't mean there can't be integration and that the old paradigm must remain.

Most of us have more imminent needs, but consider setting intentions like long-term and short-term goals. Save some of the bigger things for your visions. The more idealistic visions still require energy to be placed and propelled; they are just going to take a lot longer to accomplish. You never know where your good intentions may show up in the universe.

We've all heard stories about learning to be happy along the journey. If you haven't, find some and read them. Selfish indulgences and pleasures can be quite healing to the soul, and there is no need for guilt. Feeling guilty for things that are simply being human is clearly a third-dimensional limiting belief. Some souls came here to experience guilt and therefore need to process guilt on a deeper level. It's okay to set an intent to take better care of yourself, to have more downtime, and to have more joy. You have a body to take care of, but also allow the occasional sense pleasures. It's blatantly obvious the world needs more joy, so have joy and enjoy it, too.

Typically, you will set numerous intentions, so let's double back. Check in with the part of you that knows the truth and ask if your intention is rooted in fear, greed, or societal belief, or if your intention has a basis of peace, love, understanding, compassion, or the betterment of yourself and humanity. Your intentions can have more than one purpose. When you set an intent that betters your authentic self, allow it to be selfless. As each individual awakens and begins to take personal responsibility, we will see more of that change on a global level. From there, good intentions that become manifest can be incorporated into the collective memory. This goes hand in hand with the concept of taking not only your power back but taking our power back. Humanity needs to take the power back on a global level, and that will come from integrity and personal responsibility. We all deserve peace, comfort, and fulfillment. Along with this, we would serve ourselves and everyone most ideally if we set our intent on living our true purpose from a perspective of passion and fulfillment. So, in setting intentions, if you don't know yourself and your ego refer to chapter 10. Finding your passion and purpose that leads to fulfillment may be the first priority in your list of intentions. Oh, crap, is that on my list of intentions? Oh yeah, that's right. That's part of what led me to write even though it wasn't on the list. I'm good.

One more time, am I setting intentions that have been imposed by societal beliefs? Am I setting intentions based on what I've been told is the proper way to do things? Am I setting heart-centered intentions? What will bring me peace?

Recognize there are people around you who, because they live in a different world of belief, particularly in a world of denial, may think that you should not do something because of their own fear. Don't buy into others' fears. Don't let others tell you what to do or not to do. You may not fully understand the full impact of your intent when you first set it. Much is revealed throughout the journey. It is not important to know the depth or details. What is important is that when you are gravitating towards a passion, when you feel that tug and it feels authentic, go with it. Do you think unique individuals like Jesus or Buddha, knew their whole story from beginning to end? Allow for the possibility that the path may have twists and turns or seem to change altogether. You can go back to the original path if and when you choose. There are times when we are pulled in another direction, and it appears that we have gotten off path, only to find that the alternate route leads right back to the original path. Those moments of discovery are particularly fun and joyful.

Remember to prepare yourself for the questions by breathing love in and out, dropping your awareness into your heart and then throughout your being; expanding into your energetic field, feeling yourself grounded and divinely connected simultaneously; quieting your mind and allowing yourself to be present. In time, the time it took for things to become effortless will be meaningless and well worth the effort. There is no absolute right way. Do whatever you feel is best for you and allow things to unfold.

If you find your authentic-self coming forth, screaming, *Yes, yes, let me out!*...and find your ego retreating, content in knowing that it did its job...now is the time to discover what is truly relevant to living from a heart-centered, multidimensional consciousness and living your life as a divine being connected to all that is. This is also described as the "I AM" consciousness. Often we find that when we step into the complexity of being multidimensional, the intricacies are revealed to be simplistic. How would it feel to trust and surrender to both the simplicity and complexity and just be?

If you feel blocked, check in to see where your ego is. Does it need some consoling? With gratitude, ask your guides to intervene on your behalf and assist in removing the blocks.

76

Setting intentions creates intervention where your high council will put clues in your path but intention alone is never enough. We set intentions and are told to let go of the outcome. Too often this is where we stop. Letting go is not the end. Vision boards are a good tool and a fun exercise to do with a group of friends but you can't expect the tool to manifest your intentions. We must be in action. The action need not necessarily be specific. While we do need to let go and surrender, we sometimes fail to recognize that, once set, we are responsible for manifesting the intention. We were given will, and it's not to be used as willfulness. Find ways to act on manifesting your intention. That doesn't mean you show up with a balloon full of hot air, saying, "Watch me! I am the great and powerful Oz, and I'm going to make this happen." Think about this; the color yellow represents the solar chakra which represents your will, so why do you suppose that brick road was yellow.

Let go of the expectation that intentions must show up in a certain way. Let go of the time frame. Time is only a human experience. Linear time is a human experience. Time is only the way that our brain can rationalize and organize what we experience. Time is simply another form of energy. If you keep telling yourself that you have no time, you'll end up with no time. How many of us do this? I caught myself doing this and knew that I was creating "no time." From that knowing, I recognized that when you accomplish something by *allowing* it to happen in *its'* time—which is actually divine timing—manifestation happens in what I now call "know time." One of my guides intervened and helped me to recognize the concept of *know time* when I realized how quickly I cleared an emotional charge on something. Know time is a topic that I would love to expand on at another time, probably book two. In the meantime, when you catch yourself saying, "I have no time," stop and ask yourself if you have "no time" or "know time." Whew, too many songs coming into the idea of time; you pick.

Know time allows us to recognize what I have heard described as the time being "ripe", which I mentioned in *the preface*. Allowing things to happen, which have been perpetuated and/or manifested from your "knowing," cannot occur in other than "know time." Time, other than linear, is a really difficult concept for us to wrap our heads around, but what I have found is that in changing my perception of time, so much more has changed and moved closer to ideal.

The letting go needs to be let go of *while* we are in present action. Let go and just **be**. Let go and let be. Let go of the disappointment that comes from heavily weighted expectation. If it is meant to happen, it will happen in divine time, in the "know time." If it doesn't happen, there may be something greater that you never expected, even if it appears the spiral is taking you down further. Be not afraid. Your actions are not in vain and will lead you to something more fulfilling. Just be aware that "that something" may have been right under your nose the whole time, and you can live simultaneously in not just the "know time" but in "whole time."

Here are a few old sayings that still have value but could use a little updating:

They say "the road to hell is paved with good intentions." Hmm. Is it obvious this has something to do with not taking action? Have you created your own hell, or is hell an illusion? Take into consideration that the saying is an old way of expressing and really not the best way of propelling yourself into action. The idea of hell creates fear; fear can prevent you from taking action.

Will you really go to hell? Not likely, but it may feel that way without the right action. For some, the fear may cause them to stop setting any intentions at all. So while the old expression had value—it was a good intention because, morally, NO ONE wants to go to hell—somewhere along the line, a whisper down the lane came into play and the vibration changed. I am not judging the expression; I'm merely suggesting we correct the vibration of how the words reverberate through us. How about motivating yourself into action by imagining what it would feel like to put your intention into motion?

How about replacing that saying with; "I must not fear. Fear is the mind-killer." (Paul Atreides, *Dune*)

Patience is a virtue. Hmm? It's not about waiting for something to happen. It's about being in action and allowing things to happen in divine time, in the "know time". "Idle hands are the work of the devil." Wow! "Wait! Aren't we supposed to look before we leap?" These are sound bites that have been misconstrued over time. If you continue to take the right action, your authentic self will manifest. Let's just say, intention without action will not lead to creation or manifestation of dreams or fulfillment. Right action will create the ripples that will propel us ever closer to that which we desire.

You can't set an intention without paying attention. Paying? Paying the price? How interesting. Well, you can set an intention without paying attention, but you probably won't get too far. Personally, I really don't like the idea of what paying a price implies. Sacrifice? Martyrdom? An old paradigm past it's time? Paying attention does not come with a price, not paying attention does. Attention doesn't have a price tag because we already have it; we just have to use it. How about, instead of paying the price, we just remind ourselves that with the right action and effort, we can create something that sets us free.

Skillet—"Awake and Alive"

Chapter 8

My Mission Statement and Personal Prime Directive

Creating a mission statement can help you get really clear on your intentions to help you create a life that is more realistic and ideal. As mentioned before, in order to realize your visions, you will want to clear out the internal programming and conditioning that can cause self-sabotage. Consider all areas of your life when creating your mission statement and setting your intentions. You are welcome to use all or parts of mine (personally only) until you know what your mission and intentions are.

My mission statement:

When we learn to be consciously aware and grounded, we are living in the present moment. Our experiences are more profound, and our lives are more fulfilled. It is my sincere desire to help others create a fulfilled, fun-filled, joy-filled life, and thereby have that present in my life as well. It is my desire to help others find their own divine, intimate, direct connection to pure source.

Primary intention:

I created my primary intention (personal prime directive) because I was sick and tired of hearing people *telling* me what to do and offering contradictory advice. You must be specific. Don't be too specific. You have to ask. You have to ask the right question. You have to ask the right guide. You have to pray at ten and two because that's where you place your hands while you are driving, and who doesn't have to pray while they are driving. You have to ask for help and you have to ask for it in the right way and at the right time—11:11 or 3:33. All I could hear is: "You must pay the rent." But I can't pay the rent. "But you must pay the rent." But I can't pay the rent (*SnidelyWhiplash*). Dear God, STOP already with the limiting beliefs from people who are trying to "tell" you how to be limitless. STFU.

If I were to present to you a boiled-down short version of my primary intention, it would be this:

To master third dimension by living a harmonious and fulfilled life.

Nice and short, right? Now, the full-blown version (extreme ends of the spectrum):

I ask, intend, and desire to be divinely directly connected to the purest source of love, light, energy, information, knowledge, truth, beauty, wisdom, grace, prosperity, optimal health, wealth, harmony, happiness, joy, bliss, money, abundance, ideal physical fitness, kindness, gentleness, compassion, communication, comprehension, cooperation, passion, motivation, time, and accomplishment in any dimension or direction of time of this universe, the multiverse, and beyond, so that I may live a discernibly fulfilled, fun-filled, joy-filled life in Christed consciousness while fully grounded in this earth body. I choose to heal me, all the mes and every aspect of me in the continuum. I am the creator, the implementer, and manifestor of my ideal life, having extraordinary, tangible, present moment experiences, especially in love. I embrace the full spectrum of Martha: from the Martha that I was to the Martha that I am to the Martha that I will become—a fully integrated multidimensional being aligned in oneness and living as my authentic self.

Blessed beyond my wildest dreams, I remain ever in gratitude to God, the divine, the divine gods and goddesses, the archangels, the angels, the beings of the light, my guides, and my ancestors for their intercession on my behalf. I am grateful to any beings of divine love and light who understand the challenges of this third-dimensional world and can assist in my mastery. In turn, I share my blessings with kindness, gentleness, and compassion. I AM.

Quite a mouthful, but I wanted to cover as much as I could. I want it all. But, I want others to have it all, too. I'm good with pleasant surprises.

It's not easy to speak only from heart. That pesky ego slips in, but we can make it a goal. As humans, we needed to get knocked off balance once in a while. It keeps us humble. It helps us discover gratitude. The more we practice, the more we will remain centered, and the rough parts will be less frequent and less effecting.

Another phrase that I use often, because it resonates with me strongly is *Ayah Asher Ayah*—a phrase that came to me divinely in meditation, so I googled it. The traditional translation is this: "I am what I am." The translation I found, which is believed to be more accurate is: *I will be what I will to be*. Say that to yourself. *I will be what I will to be.* Does that create a sense of freedom for you the way it does for me? Does that offer an explanation of free will without needing another description? Does that bring up some truth to "all this I do, you shall do and more"? Breathe it in through your solar plexus, the heart of your will, and see how it feels. How is that for an intention? Clearly, this is a profound expression of the importance of our will. It provides a sense of strength, courage, integrity, and sovereignty for us to persevere in overcoming challenges. Just as every cell has a nucleus, as multidimensional beings, we have a heart in every chakra. Pieces perceived to be separate come back to the heart center to create the one, whole and complete. I typically run through my intention every day. I've said it so many times that it takes "know time" at all to get through it.

For many reasons, I felt it necessary to create my own prayer of protection. Here it is:

I claim this vessel that I occupy to be only for that which is of God's divine love and light. Anything which is not of the divine is not welcome nor has permission to enter my energetic field, nor has permission to enter the energetic fields of those that I love and surround me, nor permission to enter the space around the energetic fields or the space around the space. In this I am sovereign.

To some, it may seem odd, but when you start working with energy, you must be careful not to invite what you don't want, as you will be more susceptible through your openness if you are not protected.

Chapter 9

Mastering Third Dimension, Fear and Faith, Integrity

Part A. Mastery; Integrity and Changing Evil to Live

So what do you think? Is mastering third dimension the reason why we are here?

Does that feel right to you?

Take a few deep cleansing breaths. Surround yourself with light. Send the breath into the earth, and as you do, allow yourself to feel worthy. Send the breath up through your crown and ask for a divine connection to pure source. Surround yourself with a divine light and imagine silver and gold at the outer edges of this light. Ask yourself again, *"is mastering third dimension the reason why we are here?"*

Mastering third dimension will return us to the light, to God, god and to the oneness. How can we learn to connect to the oneness and to all that *IS*, unless we attempt while we are mastering?

Many still do not know what the ego is or give it any consideration. Consider and consideration are both words we would be wise to consider more often. Consider the saying, "Know thine enemy." How many times have you heard, "I am my own worst enemy"? Aren't we all that at some point or another? Consider what has been talked about in the concept of facing fears. Consider that our fears are of what is not known—fear of the unknown or of something that might or might not happen. A lot of us have heard the expression, "Fear is false evidence appearing real" or "false evidence altering reality." Consider that often fear turns out to be pointless but embracing fear may have revealed something you might not have otherwise known. Consider that one interpretation of "know thine enemy," is simply not knowing oneself. Shame, blame, and judgment go down the list of emotions, and they are all fear in some form. We are human; therefore, we have an ego, and fear stems from the ego. Therefore, to grow, we must turn and face our fears and face ourselves.

We must, we must, we must stop beating ourselves up. Turn and face the change. (*David Bowie*—"Changes") ("What I've Done" —*Linkin Park*)

To know ourselves, we must learn to observe ourselves. Beating yourself up over and over for something that happened in the past solves nothing. I would suggest that if the word "evil" is the opposite of "live," that evil, in this case, simply is fear holding us back from living in the present and living fulfilled.

Now, before somebody bites my head off about this, let me preface by saying, of course, evil exists in this world. We are subjected to it every day even if it's not a personal experience. I will suggest that those who appear to be evil, who have expressed evil in coming here to experience evil, chose a lesson greater than they could handle in this lifetime, and their free will was unsuccessful in finding a way back to the light. I am *not* excusing what they have done. I am not saying some shouldn't be accountable or in prison. I am simply saying that when we judge monsters, we may want to consider and find that place in our hearts that recognizes that these beings are also a creation of God. They went so far into the darkness that they are unable to find a way to the light. We also have the "beauty and the beast" metaphor to consider. Maybe they need love. Maybe the whole concept of human life is a big experiment. If we consider karma and lessons, and if we consider we have played the beast or villain in other lifetimes as part of our mastery, we might not judge so harshly. Maybe the reason why we are here is to master being human, so we can evolve. Maybe it's a test to see how much love we can learn to let shine.

Look at people who have made numerous attempts at something, initially seen as lunatics or failures, later they were vindicated, like Bruno, Galileo, even Einstein. Edison has his famous quote, "I have not failed. I've just found a thousand ways that won't work." There was doubt, ridicule, imprisonment, even martyrdom as with Joan of Arc. Likely, judgmental comments were made that he/she was "crazy" or "will never amount to anything." Strong willed, they maintained integrity, like Tesla.

Maybe the people who have expressed wickedness have just failed their chosen mission to transform evil, albeit miserably, epically, but failed? We all must develop our will to overcome evil, so we can live. Possibly, they haven't failed at all. If third dimension is an illusion as has been purported, perhaps the role of the villains in this lifetime is simply to help the rest of us to wake up, like *Caroline Myss* ("Why People Don't Heal") and *Neale Donald Walsch* ("The Little Soul and the Sun") have suggested. Maybe in another realm, they love us.

It's difficult not to question this. Forgiving monsters is hard. What we must consider is that a lot of the mess we are in comes from judgment and fear. Perhaps transforming this will transform us and we can conquer the "Kobayashi Maru." Consider, there *are* those who have appeared evil that have conquered that evil. Even if we do find it in our hearts to forgive, that doesn't mean that we shouldn't continue to combat evil, but maybe we could transform our idea of how we do battle. Of course, it is wise to question the sincerity of someone who has expressed evil and claims to have repented. Trust, particularly once broken, must be earned. While repentance sends a message of hope, we would be wise to be cautious of deceit and manipulation.

If the new agers and others who claim to say we should *just send love* actually believe this, then maybe we should have some "Sympathy for the Devil" (*Rolling Stones*). If you go back to original translations, there is debate over who Lucifer and Satan are, and if they are one and the same. How about the story of that African tribe that sings to a person when they do something against the society, because they believe the person simply forgot who they were? I've heard this credited to both the Ubuntu and the Dagara tribes. They sing that person's song to help them remember who they are. This would suggest that judgment and fear create emotions that are less than divine divine; something that all the great masters have taught. So right here, right now, I am sending sympathy to the devil, whoever or whatever that may be, even if it is only a creation of an individual who has expressed evil in this world. I hope it finds a way back to divine pure source, pure light, pure love, and find a way to live in integrity from a place of peace and understanding. Is anyone with me on this? How many stories can you remember of someone/something that appeared evil but was only seeking love?

Evil is the opposite of live.

We already know that fear is a lack of information, knowledge, acceptance and/or understanding. This is what leads to our prejudice and false judgment of others. Sadly, we have removed many topics from our classrooms and removed topics from our conversations in general just because they are uncomfortable and not politically correct to discuss when removing them is exactly what leads back to prejudice and judgment because we fear the unknown. Ignorance breeds fear. Fear breeds intolerance. Intolerance creates war. War excuses abuse and atrocity. It's mind-boggling to me and lacks common sense and common decency. How will we ever bridge the gaps in society and culture without letting go of judgment?

Integrity is the way back to the light. Personal integrity at all costs. This doesn't mean we still have to buy into the paradigm of the martyr, but it also doesn't mean that martyrs shouldn't be appreciated for what they have done for the rest of us. The martyr archetype, depending on the level to which you play it, may just set you up for drama that you don't need and don't want. Breaking down the old paradigms and programs is mastering third dimension. Once mastered, we will be in the light.

Eye for an eye doesn't work. Eye for an eye is what creates a vicious cycle of karma. Eye for an eye is created by a fear of our power being taken from us.

"An eye for an eye makes the whole world blind" (Attributed to Mahatma Gandhi).

When we live through integrity and mercy, we don't need the eye for an eye mentality. Integrity leads our journey towards peace, harmony, and unity. Karma, good or bad, keeps us stuck like a rat on a wheel? Yes, it's nice to get good karma, but the problem is that, in this world of duality, we get both and wonder why bad things happen to good people. To evolve, ultimately we could strive to end this cycle and move on to something new? Aren't you bored with the same-crap-different-day routine?

Keeping your mouth shut doesn't work when truth is being buried. Discerning the difference between when you can keep your mouth shut and when you should speak up is important. This is something we feel from the core of our body. I don't know about you, but it's profound in my being. I feel a quaking inside, like a volcano ready to erupt, when it is time for me to speak up. It's not the same as the old explosive pattern when having my buttons pushed. While it has the same intensity, it comes with a much broader awareness of passion and truth.

Speaking truth from an integrated heart sends vibrations of love around the world.

Get to know how your knowing occurs for you. Know what that feeling is and do not fear. Remain in integrity and speak your truth from your heart.

The time frame when we keep our mouth shut provides us with an opportunity to observe and to come to terms with a way to say things more appropriately, present our case, and present our side of the story in a way that is kinder and gentler regardless of whether or not it leaves a bitter taste in someone else's mouth. Reality is a bitter pill. Once we have spoken truth from the heart with ego in check, our own bitterness will be gone.

Once we have spoken our truth, the ball is in the other court, so to speak. How others respond is not your responsibility unless you were not considerate. You may have to consider that not everyone is capable or willing to accept truth, as you know it, or able to hear and speak without ego.

To be at peace, you must be willing to be detached from the outcome and accept another person's position. If you are capable of being at peace within yourself regardless of the outcome, then you are ready to act on whatever it is you have chosen to act on. If you are still in fear and don't have a sense of peace when asking yourself if you can live with any potential outcome, then you might not be quite ready to put yourself out there. Make sure it's not just discomfort of stepping out of your comfort zone, which is different from fear. That doesn't mean you can't test the waters. You might have to practice this a few times, and, more likely than not, things will backfire because of things you didn't consider. Be ready to accept the backfire. You are learning. It's bound to happen. When words of truth are given back to you from a viewpoint that you did not consider, you must remember that there are two sides to every story; they may have a perspective you didn't think of. You may have to express integrity from within yourself by offering recognition and validation and possibly an apology. That apology should be sincere with no "buts" attached.

Cliché maybe, but this is where the Golden Rule comes into play. Some of what I will say in a later chapter may appear bitter but it's not, and I make no apology for the facts or the truth.

We are always told to let go, but so many interpret that as shutting up and burying. The only burying should be the burying of the hatchet when you have reached a place of agreement or have agreed to disagree. If you can't reach that place, then you need to use the hatchet only to cut the ties.

We must reach a level of acceptance. We must reach a level of taking responsibility for experiences. That doesn't mean being the only one responsible. We must accept that somewhere in the cosmos, all this stuff was in the contract. That doesn't mean contracts can't be broken or rewritten. Your personal responsibility is the same as your responsibility to everything in life. Your main responsibility is how you respond to circumstances, situations, and people. You are responsible for maintaining your own integrity, however circumstances play out. Try to maintain, kindness, gentleness and compassion.

Primary things we must do or learn in order to master third dimension:

1. Get to know the self, get to know the ego.
2. Let go of the right fears. Let go of the fears that hold you back from living a fulfilled life.
3. Focus on breathing and awareness more often and more regularly while placing thoughts on peace. Breath and awareness leads to present moment.
4. Try to stay in the present moment as much as possible. Recognize when you are and aren't. When you get knocked off, get back on the horse named Present Moment as quickly as possible.
5. Remain in integrity.

Part B. Fear and Faith

I do believe in a higher power. I just refuse to define or label "it." I am open to the possibilities of what "it" is or even if "it" is male, female, or neither. What I know is that whatever "it" is, it is within me. My experiences have led me to this, not the teachings that were forced upon me as a child.

What is your intent for believing? Do you truly believe, or do you believe because you are afraid not to? Are you afraid of the repercussion for not believing? Believing out of fear is not true belief.

NO, NO, NO, she did NOT just say that! Boo, that's just wrong. No, it's not wrong, and, yes, I did say that. Do you believe in a higher power because of direct personal experience or out of fear?

I do have to admit that *sometimes* when a homeless person asks me for money, I am *afraid* not to give them money. My fear is they might be an angel in disguise, and I am being tested. Silly, I know. I can just hear the grumbles. Do I always give? No. But I do it randomly when spirit moves me regardless of how broke I think I am.

Just like how we have over-intellectualized consciousness and not fully incorporated it into being, so have we done with religion. I said this earlier: religion is a tool. How many religions talk about God and angels? But the stories are presented as rigid belief or myth. When a congregation member discusses a direct personal experience, they are sometimes shunned as crazy and judged behind their back. And, how about that story of the pastor disguised as homeless? True or not, it's a great story. Religion when implemented properly is valuable in creating a sense of community. Perhaps that's the real purpose behind the communion ritual. Some concepts have been taken too literally, others not literal enough. Community and communion both have *commune in* them so if we *think* about it a bit, it could be that what we need to do is commune with one another and communicate better; that doesn't mean we need to take it to the opposite extreme of communism. We could observe and consider life's spectrum to show us harmony and balance.

How many don't believe in interdimensional or intergalactic beings because they have never seen one and say there is no proof. But, they believe in a God they have never met and in the Bible, which was mostly translated in the 1400s by *men* at a time when many believed the earth was flat and still thought the sun revolved around the earth.

Too much has been hidden from us, miles of documents in fact, and there has been too much opportunity for whisper down the lane to occur. While the bible contains great information for living in integrity, maybe describing the bible as having been selectively assembled would be accurate?

It might be wise to take a closer look at what has been hidden. Does it offer moral guidelines? Yes. How about the Torah, Quran, Bhagavad Gita? Is it all true? Hmm. Probably not. Why? Because: man is flawed, and often interpretations are flawed. Should we judge anyone else's belief? Nope, we shouldn't do that either. However, too many atrocities against humanity have been and still are committed in the name of religion, including abuse, fear, or miscreation. Too much gets swept under the rug and denied to uphold the appearance of divine power. Developing consciousness and living in integrity will help us evolve beyond this.

The danger of whisper down the lane and religious conviction is exactly why I have developed a great deal of respect for people like *Dr. Neil Douglas-Klotz*, who have taken the time to translate from Aramaic, the language Jesus would have spoken. How do we definitively know what the truth is when you look at this example of interpretation: "there are just so many" (limited) or "there are just so many" (expanded)? It's the same words with two different meanings. We must find truth within ourselves.

Many profess to believe, yet they have not opened themselves up to direct personal experience. Others fear discussing a direct personal experience they had for fear of being judged. How would you respond if you met someone who claimed to be Jesus, Buddha, Krishna, Isis or Quan Yin? What if they didn't appear in solid flesh? Would you believe? How would you know? Could you be deceived? Could it be possible or true?

The more conscious you become, the clearer you get about who you really are, and the more likely you are to have that direct personal experience and be able to discern the truth. It's not that one person is better, smarter, or more deserving. It has nothing to do with any of those things. It has to do with letting go of fear, allowing and learning to discern. If you get fooled, you are not a fool. You have just been given a lesson in discernment.

True believing in anything comes from direct personal experience, for which providing proof to someone else is not required.

Reach out and touch faith and find your own "Personal Jesus" – created by *Depeche Mode* but I like the *Marilyn Manson* cover.

Part C. Fear, Addiction, Abuse

I have often pondered abuse and addiction. So many have done a great job at breaking completely free, and are to be applauded. In no way am I judging those who have an addiction which is beyond their ability to control. As for self-induced abusing, recently, I was reminded that no one becomes a substance abuser without suffering from underlying pain. However, it has been my observation that many in recovery cling to God, as if creating an all new addiction. Albeit a much wiser choice, many are unable to have a conversation without bringing up their faith in God. It seems a little codependent. Please don't sound bite me; hear me, see me, feel me, touch me, heal me. ("See me, Feel me" – *The Who*) If clinging to God prevents an addict from going backwards, then that is what they *should* do. Again, I am not judging. I've done my share of clinging, begging, and threatening, as well as being abused and self-abusing. What we must recognize is that with any form of abuse there is a need for support, and for many God is the only recognizable or reliable form of support.

To be a soldier of God, don't we need to be a little more independent? You don't see a seal or ranger having his hand held during any kind of ops. However, if you've got soul but you're not a soldier, so be it (*Killers-*, "All These Things That I've Done"). It's okay to seek peace before you concern yourself with being a peacekeeper. Let your peacekeeping begin with your army of one. True recovery comes from changing the reliance on God to reliance on god with support from God.

If there is a God, and if you believe in God as a child of God, wouldn't God ultimately want you to grow up and take responsibility for yourself? You may have to do a little self-parenting. As I recovered from abuses, I prayed a lot, but for many reasons, and while I appreciate organization, I was unable to buy into organized religion. Using alternative methods to seek truth, we all can learn to know the *I Am* connection whether you are religious or not.

As we free ourselves, we begin to feel new passions rumbling below the surface and, possibly, a desire to help others. These are different from the angry explosive rumbling of the past. Then you can pick up that phone that works two ways and say, *"Hey, God, it's me. I'm doing pretty good right now, so I'm checkin' in to see how you are?"* Stop a moment and ask how that would feel. You may take a breath automatically. *"I was thinkin' that, uh, maybe I could lift a little burden off of you, if you want!"* Could this be one possible path to salvation? Could this be a path to fulfillment and mastery?

Maybe you aren't there yet. Maybe you are still in pain or angry. Maybe you feel like God has let you down or abandoned you. Are you still asking all the whys? Been there, done that. Just imagine for a moment what it would feel like if you were ready to let go of the pain, the anger and the whys. Just get on the path and ride. No path? Cut your own. I remember praying; "teach me to walk a Christed path." Why didn't I ask to ride rather than walk? Oui! While I denied rigid religious belief, I did not deny the maker. (*Alice in Chains,* "Man in the Box") I just refuse to define who or what that is. Find that disturbing? Maybe for all of us to wake up to the truth of humanity, we need to be disturbed. Some of you might not like this song choice, but it is about abuse "Down With the Sickness" – *Disturbed*.

Here's the thing that can happen with recovery from any type of abuse. If you label yourself, it is what you will continue to be. If you label yourself as a substance abuser, you will continue to be a substance abuser. If you continue to label yourself as a victim of sexual, child, or spousal abuse, you will continue to be a victim. There's a good possibility that once you stop labeling yourself, you may be ready to take the leap of faith, and the step will appear. This metaphor was used in *Indiana Jones and the Last Crusade*. It's our quest for the Holy Grail. This is the step towards detaching from God but never being separate from God where we find true power with humility and humbleness. We *all* can become the Christ consciousness. Not already being there doesn't mean you are not worthy, nor does it make you entitled. With sovereignty, we can all state, "I am no longer a victim, I am no longer abused, and I am not an abuser. I am not my past."

Again, religion is a tool, it's not the end-all and be-all. It can be a guiding light, but it is not the only guiding light. Some people need it; some don't. Going to a service can guide you to a direct connection to divinity, but the connection comes from inside of you. This correlates to the message that Jesus gave us about the *"kingdom being inside us and all around us,"* as well as the message *"the most high does not dwell in houses made with hands."* I suspect we are victims of sound bites, not only because of mistranslations but in the times when many of the messages were written, they didn't have computers to write, rewrite, and edit. Who is to say that all the found manuscripts were the final edit or that the writing wasn't being used as a tool like journaling? Many wrote while in fear of censorship, so clues may have been obscured and subsequently misinterpreted. You have the right to choose to believe or not believe, and that includes whatever your idea of God is. Connections exist, whether you believe or not.

If you are conscious and have a conscience, the only judgment you will face when you get to heaven is the judgment you place upon yourself.

If you don't quite have yourself under control with abuse and addiction, I would suggest you stay tethered to God and prayer until you do. You also might want to try meditating. Take the step into the unknown when you are ready. Get to know yourself well enough to know when you are. You might want to let go of the expectation that everyone has the same religious belief as you do.

None of this makes me or anyone else a heretic where we have to sacrifice ourselves and be imprisoned for what we believe. In today's world, it may not be so much a jail cell as it is a self-imposed prison related to the message I was given—"release your self-imposed burdens"—that I told you about in Chapter 1. The message offers a bit more enlightenment, peacefulness, and open-heartedness with less judgment and can offer stronger faith.

These are the keys and tools to save yourself and to keep you out of suppression. Everything contains an element of reason. Everything happens for a reason. Common sense will prevail if you let it. You choose what you wish to see or not see. Knowing comes in the form of choosing to see the truth for what it is. I've had many direct personal experiences with Jesus and several beings of divine light. Today, many others have, too, and it's okay to step forth and say so. "She Talks to Angels" – *The Black Crowes.*

Chapter 10

Know Thyself

Part A. Getting to Know You

Well it seems if you just take the title of this section and look up the song and make the song about you, you don't need to read the rest of this section. Humpf. Musicals just aren't my style but what powerful words the song "Getting to Know You" (*Rogers and Hammerstein*) contains.

How will we ever know our dreams, desires, goals, wishes, and purpose unless we truly know ourselves?

Getting to know all aspects of you, the full spectrum, the ego, the personality, and dare I say limits from the aspect of what you are willing and/or not willing to do will create an understanding within yourself of yourself that makes acceptance, letting go, and forgiveness, along with the manifestation of your dreams much easier.

No matter what is going on in the outside world, it is important to be comfortable in your own skin. You have to live with you, and you are closer to you than anyone else so why wouldn't you want to be friends with you?

**Caution: Don't use "that's just how I am" or "this is what I do" or "I have this or that issue" as an excuse to stay stuck in the past, wallow in self-pity, perpetuate self-loathing or remain arrogant for that matter.

What you do is not who you are.

Ironically, I found myself in a profession that a lot of people view on par with used car salesmen. When my clients would get annoyed with something that they did not want to hear, I would say, "This is what I do, not who I am." That statement took the edge off of the conversation and created a level of trust.

Knowing who you are and what you want are two different things. How can you absolutely know what you want with no uncertainty unless you know who you are? Don't let that be a set up to a fear of making mistakes. Knowing what you want can help you get to know who you are. You can make what you do a part of you, but it is not you.

Know thyself is mentioned in many philosophical studies: Egyptian, Greek, Buddhism, Qabala and more. I admit that I haven't made a full study of this. What I know is that the idea resonates for me. My inward journey has taught me what I need to know on this topic. I also know that the guy that *Bill and Ted* refer to as "So-Crates" comes into play somewhere.

Through awareness and observation, you can correct behaviors that are less than ideal. No disrespect intended for anyone named Dick, but the fact is we call people dicks, so this is my tribute to the characters *Dick Solomon* and *Dean Winchester.* If you want to beat yourself up a little for acting like a dick, go ahead. Admit you were a dick. Embrace that you were a dick. By embracing it, you can accept it, forgive yourself and let it go. This doesn't mean you should learn to love being a dick so much that you perpetuate being a dick and not apologize for being a dick. Sometimes we just don't know what we just don't know and that includes knowing what it's like to be a dick and not be a dick. In knowing yourself, your ego won't be offended by what others say or think because you will know the real truth of who you are and who you aren't. In turn you can give yourself a pat on the back for your admirable qualities without being an arrogant dick. Some of my best lessons have come from a real friend not being afraid to tell me that I was being a dick. Why? Because: I wasn't even aware I was being a dick, and don't want to be a dick unless it's all in fun. That doesn't mean you make a habit of going around telling people they are dicks because that's just going to make you look like a bigger dick.

I have a friend who was very wrapped up in healing through feeling to the point of overkill. She took it very seriously and it would upset her deeply when I teased her. Finally, I said "if you don't like being teased, just say f- you Martha, shut up." Suddenly, there was a shift from overemotional feeling to thinking. She had been trapped in her idea of feeling. Thinking hadn't occurred to her. It turned into a hysterically funny moment and a profound discovery of wisdom. We learned much about ourselves and each other. Ego was dropped, everything became lighter, a deeper, more intimate bond was formed, clarity shone through and awareness created soul recognition.

To me, this is a clear example of why we *should* bother to get to know ourselves, integrate our thinking and feeling, and learn to regularly live from heart-centered knowing. Getting to know what *you know* will open doors to intimacy within yourself and creates a bridge to intimacy with others. There are times when feeling has more relevance and times when thinking has more relevance, but the integration of the two leads to authenticity and deeper knowing.

To be clear and concise, there is a difference between emotions and feeling. Get to know the difference between yours. Emotions are not bad. Some are good but others hold you hostage, which is exactly why you need to get to know your ego and help it to grow up.

In knowing who you are, how you think, and feel it makes it easier to figure out what you want. Knowing does not completely negate the trial, error, success process; it eliminates the drama. Knowing yourself makes you more proficient in acting on what feels natural. Knowing helps you remember who you really are, not the illusion of who you are, which leads to a more fulfilling life.

Do you have a hard time making choices? Do you have a hard time asking for help? Are you helpful or helpless? Do you find yourself stuck in I-don't-knows? Do you think that to get something done right, you have to do it yourself? Do you fear mistakes? Do you know your boundaries? Is your patience too thick or too thin? Are you confident or overconfident? Are you filled with self-doubt? Do you think or feel before you speak? How often do you find yourself reacting or overreacting rather than responding graciously from the heart? Do you know how to utilize your filter? What sets you off? What do you avoid? What should you avoid? Do you know how to apologize? Does your ego fear apologies? Do you know when it's important to apologize and when it's not? In book two, I plan to do a whole chapter on the art of apology. What situations stress you out? What brings you joy? What brings a sense of wanting to say yes? What makes you smile? Where do you see beauty? When can your remember a time that felt timeless? What makes you cry with sadness? What makes you cry with joy? What makes you cry, simply because it touches your heart? Have you ever taken the time to know what it feels like to speak from the heart? These questions are just a few examples for you to explore. Learn to ask for help in areas where you have weaknesses, and offer your strengths in exchange.

****CAUTION: Don't be overwhelmed with so many questions that it becomes idle chatter or chaos.*

We must get to know what makes us FEEL: the good and the bad, the perfect and the not so perfect, your strengths and weaknesses, fine points and flaws, or your yin to your yang. You may already have a yin to your yang outside of you, but finding it inside creates a more desirable bond with yourself and your world. In knowing the self, you discover your purpose, live that purpose, live purposefully, and fulfilled. Ya think? Ya feel? Ya know?

Some are lucky and have a clear path from the day they are born. Most of us have to figure it out. Hell, I still don't know what I am going to do when I grow up. Maybe I just won't. We can choose to follow a distinct path or continue to explore new things. But that doesn't mean we have to be a lost boy.

Knowing yourself propels you in the direction of choices and opportunities. It's also okay to pass when something doesn't feel right or important. Not every choice will appear to be right, but they won't be all wrong.

Once you have a good grasp in knowing yourself, you can laugh even in the midst of the suckiest situation. Instead of diving into the poor-me side of your ego and wallowing around, you can laugh and say, "I am having a bad day; I need a pity party." Give yourself a 5 second pity-party and move on. In knowing yourself, nothing is such a big deal that it can't be overcome. Remind yourself that you are okay.

It's sad when you see someone get angry, and you know that they are only angry because they don't know their authentic self, and are unable to express honestly from a heart-centered consciousness. The anger comes from the ego, which is trying to protect them from their insecurities. On the flip-side there are times when someone should get angry and ego holds them back, also from insecurity. If you know yourself, you will be strengthened, and so will your ability to express. Willfulness and pride will disappear; that false evidence appearing real will disappear.

Learn to enjoy the illusion at least a little; play with the illusion until you become that master magician of your story. Then play some more.

Know thyself. Get to know yourself on a deeper level, all aspects. Observe how the ego reacts, but don't use it as an excuse to stay the same. When our ego plays the trickster, it does so for a reason. Don't say, "That's just how I am" or "I am too old to change" or "My upbringing prevents me from thinking differently." You ALWAYS have a choice. "I'm too old" or "I don't have time" is an excuse.

We are not just one way or another. Wait, I think I just heard *Blonde's* "One Way or Another," but don't go there yet. The point is we are multidimensional beings interconnected to the oneness. This is not just some airy-fairy crap, which, at times, has been made to look that way by people who live in fear of the unknown. Knowing yourself creates internal stability and integrity when used wisely.

In knowing your ego, you will know when it needs to be put into a time out, when it needs to be told to sit on the bench, when it can come out to play, when it can sit in the front row of the audience, when it needs a nap, when it needs to retire, and when it needs to be honored. It has been there to assist you even when it acts like a brat and should grow up. It's a part of you. Appreciate it, accept it, and allow it to share the joy of your progress. Embrace it with love and thank it for its support. Let it revel with you as you reach fulfillment, let it see all the blessings of freedom, and let it retire in peace. Let it smile in friendship at your authentic self as it turns over the reins of power.

Part B. Big Egos

Growing up, I only ever heard about ego in terms of being "a big ego" and that of being less than admirable. As children, how would we know that the ego contained multiple facets, let alone that one existed? Psychology was definitely not on the list of topics at my house. In fact, if you brought it up, you were told you had rocks in your head. After all, there wasn't anything that a good crack in the ass wouldn't fix. Uh-huh? Right? Does anyone else hear the multiple aspects of fear and ego there? I don't want to mislead. I was not physically abused by my parents. My dad's angry, almost disembodied threats, along with the gruff cigarette-smoking voice; my mom's poor-me, served up with guilt gravy; and both with stern convictions was enough to scare the crap out of me and make me feel like I was in a constant tug-of-war. Beyond that, their attention was only on the physical. It was assumed and expected that you think exactly like them.

I remember attempting to talk things out, gain understanding or get advice. The typical answer was "you're doin' all the talkin'." What kind of answer is that?

Because of the preconceived notion of "big ego," I didn't even know that we all had an ego, let alone multiple aspects. What I perceived was that you either had a big ego or you had no ego at all. Since we often perceive people with big egos as assholes, I surely didn't want to be that even though I can be an ass at times. Being exposed to this attitude creates a fear of success on the inside even though, outwardly, you go through the motions of moving toward success. It sets up unconscious self-sabotage. I perceived that successful people, who outwardly seemed to have it all, the ones my mom and *Billy Joel* call the "Big Shot(s)," had deep dark secrets, as if they had all sold their souls to the devil. While I hadn't sold my soul to the devil, I had some deep dark secrets, and there was no way I was going to risk letting them out.

No wonder so many ego-centric people rise to power, while the better qualified stay behind. I sense this could be why the world is such a mess. Getting to "know thyself" should be added to ALL school curriculum, along with nondenominational meditation and mindful awareness. Really, how does a moment of silence hurt anyone even if you are an atheist? It doesn't! Science proves that meditation keeps us healthier, more focused, and less stressed. Who said that a moment of silence has to be about religion? It doesn't. It's just another example of blind stupidity from egomaniacs.

Okay, time for Martha to take a breath and blow it out. How about a moment of silence for peace? I can get so mad. Is that my ego? Nah, that's about injustice. Injustice is about lack when lack is unnecessary when common sense is exercised. I need to listen to *David Bowie's* passion to calm me down. Oh, wait! That's "Fashion." Never mind. But that would still be a good break song.

Okay, we are back. Did you dance? Our education system is not creating a world of wonder or passion, because with passion and wonder comes excitement, and we certainly can't have any excitement in school. Oh no, kids are told to sit down and shut up. If you stay quiet, you fall through the cracks. If you show any excitement, you are going to be labeled and drugged. Shouldn't there be more teaching on what energy is and how to channel it?

With the prevalence of this in society today, who doesn't know someone who has been labeled with this ADD or ADHD? My daughter has a friend who has been labeled. The thing is that this kid is a brilliant guitar player. He spends hours listening, learning and practicing. At 14, he won a contest in front of approximately 30,000 people. If he were really an ADHD and couldn't focus, then how could he focus so much attention on learning guitar? School simply doesn't offer a place where kids can learn from the heart, their own unique divine nature, their own place of wonder and excitement. We hear about this kind of frustration a lot. Forget about asking questions. Do the lesson and answer from the system's perspective.

If you question the way history was written, you can get kicked out for being a troublemaker. I've seen this happen too. Even Winston Churchill said, "History is written by the victors." Obviously, this means it's only written from one perspective, ignoring any other point of view or the other side of the story. "Might" doesn't make "right" when the bully is the winner. Some circumstances are pretty clear that removing a lunatic from power was necessary, but how many times have stories been told solely from the viewpoint of the bully who, too often, is romanticized: Cleopatra, Alexander the Great, and Genghis Khan.

How can kids know themselves and become independent beings when they are being suppressed and not supported? As adults, we often wish we still had the energy we had when we were kids. Why suppress it? The overall system is not inspirational. Instead, it inspires an attitude of "why bother"? It works for the needs of the few who are okay with right-brain conformity, but it's failing the needs of the many, as evidenced by our falling global position. While there are many who are doing the best that they can, it's also very dysfunctional.

Whose brilliant idea was it to impose so many prescription drugs because kids are full of energy and have a short attention span? Um, excuse me, but isn't it scientific knowledge that the brain doesn't mature until twenty-five years of age? Granted, there are genuine cases where drugs help, but the over-prescribing of drugs to our kids is a blatant abuse, especially when we are telling them to say no to drugs. Here again, contradiction without a coherent explanation.

As a parent, we have the right and responsibility to talk to our kids; to get to know our kids; to teach them to use their own intuition so that together you can make choices that will help them to grow up to be better balanced, more responsible adults, as they continue to play the game of life. Teach them that they have choices. Guide them to make better ones and don't emotionally crucify them when they don't. Teach them to think, feel and know themselves, for themselves.

We are all more inspired to learn when lessons have value, meaning, and purpose. We all learn when we are interested. Sometimes we have to be exposed to purpose, value, and practical application. Some of our kids and some of us have simply chosen a path that appears to be unconventional and people with big egos fear that. ADD, ADHD is an overused label created out of fear of the unknown which is turning out to be suppressive and abusive. I'm not saying kids don't need to be reminded to stay on a path, but we should not expect them to conform to a dysfunctional system.

I hear frustration from parents regularly, who want something better, but are still trying to make their kids conform because of their own conditioning. Why?

We have to teach our kids to be conscious. By not suppressing them, they can be our teachers. We should not try to live vicariously through them. It doesn't mean you shouldn't guide them, support them, or love them. Nor does it mean you should give them too much rein. When you ride a trail horse, you guide in the direction you want to go. But once you are on the trail, you give the horse its head, you loosen the rein, and you let them pick their steps. This is natural. This is not forced. This is cooperation. If you force a horse in a direction other than what is natural, it may stumble and fall. It may stumble and fall on its own, but it will occur less often. At some point, you need to get off its back and give it a rest. This is what we need to do with our kids—get off their backs. When you give them the rein, they will succeed even if they need you to ride their back once in a while. No one intentionally sets out to fail, but too often the system sets us up for failure.

I know that the cheer, "stand up, sit down, fight, fight, fight" is meant to inspire winning attitude, but...if you step back, look at the words, and listen to the words, you may notice a different take on it. We are telling our kids to stand up and sit down, do what they are told, and to never express any creativity or free thought but go to war and fight for something, even if they don't know what they are fighting for, because we taught them not to question.

Look, I am not trying to say that a good ass whooping doesn't have any merit. Sometimes a bully could use a good ass whooping if it provides shock value to wake them up to change their ways. And I know that "try, try, try" isn't much of a cheer, but I think you see my point. Words have vibration. Those vibrations impact all of us.

Why did I feel that information on the education system belonged under the section on big egos? Because: the system and people who control the system with big egos are attempting to force conformity on all of us which is creating the zombie mentality. It's the dumbing down of America, and it's quite evident. We need to wake up and recognize when our ego is hurting and not helping.

I so miss *George Carlin*. To highlight one of his rants; "The owners of this country…don't want well-informed, well-educated people capable of critical thinking…That's against their interest…They want obedient workers…people who are just smart enough to run the machines and do the paperwork, and just dumb enough to passively accept all these increasingly shittier jobs."

How's this for a little revival? "Teach Your Children" by *Crosby, Stills, Nash, and Young*

Part C. Wounded Egos

Moving on to the other side of the spectrum, we have the wounded ego. The wounded ego can really create some damage. The ego gets squashed before the authentic being is allowed to blossom. This is where the poor-me and the victim personality develops. Ego is a whole study into itself, but you don't have to turn your journey into one. However, if you truly desire to come from a heart-centered consciousness, spend a little bit of time learning about the ego and how to use it properly. In the discovery process of your own ego and learning to ask yourself which feelings come from your heart and which emotions are coming from the ego, you will respond more authentically to any situation. This includes situations where you recognize that you did not initially respond well. Knowing yourself will allow you the courage to step up and admit to your shortcomings. In doing so, you may discover that your relationships becoming more intimate.

Intimacy allows us to feel connected. Be intimate with yourself. Be both, the participant and the observer. This integrates the whole-self. Lack of integration with the whole-self creates the illusion of feeling disconnected, alone and wounded. Integrate or disintegrate. Are you getting this? Participating with mindful awareness develops your mastery.

In communicating with someone who does not understand the ego, keep in mind that when you try to explain to them that you see the ego side of a problem they are describing to you, they may end up with hurt feelings, because of even suggesting they have an ego. Been there done that multiple ways. These are the people who say, "I mean, you know," but have no clue what they are trying to "I mean, you know" say.

Your brain and your ego are part of your human experience. Often, in our youth, our ego provides us with drive and motivation and offers a glimpse of discovering our purpose, whether from being wounded or from being large.

Stop wronging your ego. Often when we begin to learn about the ego, someone will say, "That's just your ego." The tendency is to immediately wrong the ego. We need to hear to the whole clip: "That's just your ego trying to help and protect you." By not understanding the whole clip, we invalidate a part of self. By not expressing the whole clip, we risk invalidating others. This is particularly damaging to someone with a wounded ego. Find a way to recognize the ego more kindly and compassionately. In doing so you may discover more kindness and compassion for yourself and others. Obviously, the sentence does not need to be completed if you already comprehend this, but what if someone doesn't? Honor your ego for what it has done. Once known, your ego comes up to show you a better way to communicate and express because you have validated it. Now, you can filter your words before they come out of your mouth and express more clearly, concisely from the heart. That doesn't make the feeling that came up or the ego wrong. It's all in how you use it.

Integration of the ego provides strength and courage to move in whatever direction will create fulfillment. Tell it has done a fantastic job, but now your authentic self is strong enough to shine through and take charge. Your ego has battle scars. When are you going to let it rest so the wounds can heal and not be reopened? Tell the ego it is welcome to come forward if it has new wisdom to share. The ego is a master teacher; your authentic self is the master, the Kwisatz Haderach. (Reference to Frank Herbert's – *Dune*, the "Supreme Being.")

Now let's listen to *Stone Temple Pilots* –"Creep".

Chapter 11

Personal Responsibility

No matter what, maintain integrity with yourself, with others, and anything that you do. If more people took personal responsibility, there would be much less conflict and drama in the world.

When you start to integrate your body, mind, and spirit, and especially your ego, you will automatically begin to live in integrity. When you live in integrity, you may begin to automatically integrate. Willingly you accept personal responsibility—something that is largely lacking today and something we've already touched on *a lot*. Again this is not about blame in either direction; yourself or others. It's about being better, not perfect, better.

Your main responsibility is how you respond to circumstances, situations, and people. You are responsible for maintaining your own integrity.

When you take charge and take personal responsibility for your life, you will learn to communicate more clearly and express more freely, and with that you will learn a new meaning of "cooperation." The universe will have no choice but to allow joy into your life. A really good "why bother."

When you take personal responsibility, you let go of a lot of complaining and blaming, and you will choose to participate in a lot less drama. In turn, you simply won't attract as much.

When you take personal responsibility, you will live in less denial and more accountability.

When you take personal responsibility, you put responsibility where it belongs, and that isn't always with you.

When you put personal responsibility where it belongs, it reduces self-imposed burdens, which, in turn, will make your efforts more effortless because sabotage has been removed.

When you accept personal responsibility, you let go of expectations and set morals and standards for yourself without placing judgment on others.

When you accept personal responsibility, you take charge of your life. You know your own strengths and weaknesses, and you accept responsibility for what you can and can't do. You accept responsibility for saying yes or for saying no, and you hold yourself accountable when you fail. You are able to accept success graciously.

Personal responsibility has been a big soap box for me. I take it pretty seriously on all levels, so I have to remind myself not to take it so seriously from time to time and have more fun. Personal responsibility includes responsibility for how you feel, the way you express, respond, interact and enjoy life.

Unlike the person that...forget it! That would just be complaining, blaming, and pointing the finger. We must learn to detach when our reality isn't someone else's, but we certainly don't have to participate in someone else's' irresponsibility. If only we could find a way to do this with the government.... Okay, so maybe we don't always have a choice not to participate when something is imposed upon us by irresponsible imbecilic politicians. But maybe if we all start to become more conscious and responsible, we would experience a shift.

We've all heard "be the change you want to see." Here, again, we intellectualize that and shout, "Hell yeah," but then what? Often we are so busy, distracted, unaware, and/or not grounded that we don't give it another passing thought. And, by not giving it attention, it slips into the dark side, rather than being given sunlight and roots where change can take hold and grow. Grounded, roots, sunlight from above, growth? This is why it is so important to be grounded and divinely connected at the same time. It's wonderful to have your head in the clouds and dream, but for change to be tangible, we must be responsible for nurturing change. Take that dream in the clouds and give it a root. Question yourself. If you are nurturing change, then FANTASTIC, kudos to you. If not, ask yourself, "Where could I be accepting more personal responsibility?" It could be anywhere—in relationships, your own health, finances, or happiness, etc. Are you in complete integrity in answering yourself without an imposed belief? Tap into the knowing within and imagine love surrounding you when you do.

While we are finishing up, here is a profound example of a song meant to inspire; *Eric Clapton's*—"Change the World."

I think, I believe, and I feel that the concept of "be the change" is a great one. However, we are seeing change every day that we don't necessarily want. We are still miscreating so many things. We are responsible to stand up for ourselves and to cooperate at the same time. That doesn't mean you always have to rebel or conform, but you can make a responsible choice to do the right thing. We can choose opposites in harmonic contrast or opposites as in "opposition." If we all could be more responsible in moving our world closer to ideal by letting go of entitlement or its opposite of unworthiness, justice just might begin to prevail over our miscreations. Truth and justice? Is a Justice League just fantasy? Not if we all take more responsibility, let go of playing the victim or the villain, and learn how to live responsibly in integrity.

Sometimes things have to get worse before we say enough and they get better. While things could always get worse, there is no reason to push ourselves towards genocide or suicide. Personal responsibility will lead us to something that is more *just*, more like the idea of Camelot—a place where a rich man can easily "pass through the eye of a needle" and take justice with him. If there are two sides to everything, then it is entirely possible that we can all begin to act more responsibly beyond being responsible for our alcohol consumption.

Chapter 12

It's Not All about You— Two Sides to Every Story

To prepare for this chapter listen to *Tool*–"Right in Two"

It's not all about you. I wish I could teach my cats this. I guess they have past-life memories of being gods in Egypt or on a faraway planet, so they just don't care. It's okay. I love my cats and dogs.

For me, to remain in integrity, I must keep my ego in check and remember that this book is not all about me. But since there are two sides of every story, and if I am going to help, I have to reveal a little bit about my direct personal experiences as tangible examples.

A long time ago, someone told me, "It's not all about you." Can't remember where I heard it first. Regardless, it stuck with me, and I have been preaching it ever since. It's easy to see in business, but not so much with those whom we are close because, sometimes, we are too close to see the whole picture of what is happening. In dealing with those who are close to us, if we are pushing too hard, we need to back off a bit and observe. In doing so, often something magical will be revealed. Even if we are not pushing, we still need to back off to gain a new perspective, acceptance, understanding and compassion, Have you ever caught yourself expressing compassion for a stranger but not for someone close to you? Knowing there are two sides and it's not all about us helps in letting go of judgment and allows us to forgive even if "they" don't. It leads us towards compassion regardless of our opinions.

In this concept of "it's not all about you," we can clearly see that we have the inner and outer world of self, the inner and outer world of family, and the inner and outer world outside of home. In business—say, you are dealing with someone who is angry, irate, or just plain not nice—it is easy to see that it's not about you. If you did everything you could to be helpful, and it wasn't accepted, let it go. You have no idea what else is going on in that person's life, period. Keep your ego out of it. You can still offer kindness. And, face it, we are a planet of talking monkeys; no disrespect to monkey's intended. The animal kingdom often shows more kindness that humans do. You don't deserve to be someone else's punching bag, and knowing that it's not about you makes your ability to handle situations more tolerable or have no effect at all.

Honestly, I've been practicing this one for so long that I rarely ever attract that type of behavior anymore in any area...except for the one time I needed to have something reflected back to me that I was doing at home. Wow! That's the day I took personal responsibility, implemented some changes in me, ritually cleaned the house as a resolution towards change, and, with integrity, apologized for my behavior. That's what happens when you come from your heart, put the ego in time-out, let go of conditioning, and not just accept conditions as they are. I am no longer a victim, so I no longer play a victim, and I sure as hell don't want to be a victimizer. The change did not go unnoticed or unappreciated, and I did not overcompensate out of guilt. I simply and justly changed things to a way that was more harmonious for everyone.

Life *is* a two-way street. It would benefit us to experience give-and-take, proving that it's not all about you or all about me. Look at the other side. Walk in another person's shoes but don't abuse them. Sometimes we resonate strongly with the Golden Rule, and so rigidly hold onto it with our convictions, that we focus on the grip and fail to set the rule free.

I always conveyed the "it's not all about you" message to others, especially in the work environment, and it always helped. I know a few who will attest to that. The other preachy message that I used was the "two sides to every story." I preached it so much it's no wonder I have to include it. Hmm. Practice what you preach. If you dish it out, you better learn to take it. If I dish out integrity, will I get integrity? If I serve up personal responsibility and accountability, will I experience that in others? Sorry, I was just thinking out loud there...I mean, on paper or computer. There's still a sound bite in there somewhere, and a tone of two sides in the presentation of the words. I'll let you figure it out. Back to business.

In keeping with my intent to show how we can translate inward knowing to the outward world, here is a story to share. One day, while at one of my illusory/real world job, I overheard this heated argument occurring on the phone with another person in our service department. I politely asked the person in my office to put the call on hold. I picked up the phone, and I simply explained, "We don't know what things look like on your side; we only know what things look like from our side. So it would help all of us to be more efficient and get along better if we had an understanding of how things worked on your side, so that we can provide you with what you need and make both our jobs easier." There was a moment of silence and, suddenly, there was an atmosphere of calm and cooperation, as well as a big attitude change every time we dealt with this individual from there forward.

Now, this may seem simplistic, but it is the epitome of the "there are two sides to every story" theme.

So, in this big theme that I latched onto a long time ago in this galaxy—there are two sides to every story—*somewhere in between is the truth*. It's particularly helpful in letting go of the need to defend oneself, letting go of the need to be right, and letting go of caring what other people think. It also teaches us not to judge when we only hear one side of the story. When you really learn to discern because of the knowing you have developed in coming from a heart-centered consciousness, your knowing will reveal the truth or, magically, the truth will find a way of revealing itself to you. And you can feel gratitude in many areas and on many levels. The whole premise of the "two sides" statement has an air of common sense, and so does speaking from your heart. Well, your heart doesn't have lips, but you know….

Of course, the truth is still subjective to perception and interpretation. In the "two sides" theme, we don't always know the other person's perspective. They may be thinking something that never occurred to us. Maybe your perspective never occurred to them. All you can do is to be open, honest, and free.

In dealing with any relationships, you must decide what you can live with and what you can't. You will need to decide when to hang on, when to let go, and when to make a fast getaway. Learn tolerance and intolerance and all its counterparts. Often rough spots are lessons for which you will be stronger after. Learn to recognize what is your issue and what is theirs. This is when *truly* knowing yourself comes in handy, and even if you don't shake hands with the other party/parties, you can reach a truce within yourself. Know thyself and your limitless limitations. Wow, what an oxymoron! Yet it's true. Learn to know when you can live with your choices, because regret really sucks. We all make choices. And it would be wiser to be able to accept and respect others' choices, especially when their choice is not the one that you would make. This may be common sense, but it's amazing how often you encounter perceived intimate relationships where one knows very little about the other.

Often, in the story of the butterfly, we immediately take pity on the butterfly, recognizing the value in our need for struggle so that we can become whole and strong. What we tend to overlook is the other side of the story and how the man is feeling. Oh, that's right. Men don't have feelings. Just kidding! I do not advocate male bashing. It's not just the butterfly's need for struggle. The story has many more elements on the man's side, like regret, patience, and guilt. How often do we look at that side? In real life we often choose a side due to our own emotional attachment without really looking at all the facts and this is when the victim can sometimes get a raw deal.

In recognizing that it's not all about you, we can see that everything is just an experience, and it is an opportunity for growth with no need to take things so personal. When you are with certain people and there is a pattern where you feel your ego rearing its ugly side and you begin to take things personally, recognize that these situations are toxic. You may not want to continue with this pattern. Walk away. Run away. Be careful of what follows. (*U2* – "I Will Follow")

"Go where you are celebrated, not where you are tolerated."—Unknown

On the other hand, there is always another side of the story. Sometimes there can be a truce. Other times, even if you think you know someone, they might not know themselves or be willing to face themselves. Their ego is in the way. You might never know the truth, and it doesn't really matter.

It only matters when someone is falsely accused and imprisoned unjustly. If you have been accused but not imprisoned, then unchain yourself and release yourself from the self-imposed prison. Go and create new bonds that do matter. Create bonds that don't put you in handcuffs. There are things that are just not acceptable, just not okay. Use your tools to create things that are better than okay, maybe even extraordinary.

If you need support, find a way to get it. Remember that people who we have been conventionally conditioned to believe are the ones who will give us support, may not be capable of offering it. That means you may have to get it outside of your biological family and get it professionally and etherically.

Everything on this physical plane can be equated to something metaphoric. For me, I had no idea how championing an issue on environmental toxicity would lead to championing the issue of environmental toxicity within myself. Pay attention to the synchronicities in your life. It was in championing something that wasn't about me where I found the support I needed personally.

Holding on to the good and letting go of the bad, I hold the feelings gifted to me by those who supported me. Thank you. You remain in my heart; all of you. I am grateful to those who didn't support me. You showed me the difference. And thank you to those who have accused or hated me because you didn't know the whole story or the truth in between. You have shown me a whole new dimension of truth. Thank you to those who could not face me, it gave me the courage to set myself free.

I am amazed how divinely guided this book has been, because I have been offered physical reminders of my journey every step of the way.

My spiritual journey has evolved to a point where I spend time going through life with both eyes wide open yet connected to the oneness through my third eye. We can all do this. Our two eyes can show us both sides of the story; our third eye shows us the connectedness of the two sides. There are times when we must shut our eyes, turn our back, and walk away. But very few things are ever black and white, and there are shades of grey to consider. The truth in between is where we experience color and accept diversity.

When we begin to see the color, we often find peace. So if you have a teen who wears all black, it's not necessarily a sound for alarm. It could be for some, but for others, don't worry. They've just chosen to start with a blank canvas, and they will place the light, the sound, and the color, and dance to their own rhythm. A cocoon is often one color but the Butterfly is brilliant. Let the cocoon open when it's ready. Just keep it in a nurturing environment and away from toxicity. As an adult, you can rebirth yourself while you are here. You don't have to leave the planet. Seriously, there is a technique called rebirthing so you have a choice to rebirth, physically, metaphorically or both. You may have a better understanding of self, and you can create a whole new facet of you. If others can't see that, so what! You do! You will be a better parent to yourself when you know yourself.

My choice to move, made from a sensation of move or die, was initially viewed by me only from a perspective of physical body health, though deep inside I knew I was guided to move to heal my entire being. My move was met with controversy and struggle. The toxicity that surrounded both my inner and outer world fought desperately to cling to me. It tried to falsely accuse me and keep me in prison. What I didn't see, until I was free, was just how much value leaving meant to me. Ayah, Asher, Ayah; "I will be, what I will to be." My will drove me before I could feel my heart. My intellect drove me. My high heart, my discernment, and my internal knowing created a bridge in both directions that led to the heart. This is how I know that we have a heart in each chakra; many hearts are beating as one and the truth is at the main heart center. Tapping into the hearts in each chakra kept me going. Until you feel from your heart, you remain in opposition, feeling the struggle between the two sides of self. Once you fully comprehend the two sides and the two collide, you can begin to recognize the dimensions beyond. As Jesus said, "Be in it, not of it." This is when you integrate all aspects of yourself, and you will grasp the meaning without gripping too tightly.

I wasn't always certain if my ability to see things from both sides was a blessing on a curse. I am clear on that now. It is a blessing. I attempt to approach everything from this perspective and from a perspective of open-heartedness, because I have more knowledge on how to stop the penetration of the slow-blade attacks. While we all have physical bodies, not everything is physical and not everything is metaphoric or spiritual—it's a combination. It is in gaining new perspective that we can reach understanding, communication, cooperation, appreciation, compassion and more. We simply have to be *willing*. Although accused of being a troublemaker, the truth is I am a peacemaker. The thing is that I have had to accept that I can't bring peace to everyone in this time line. Maybe it will happen in the "know time." In the meantime, I will find a place of acceptance. It doesn't matter that everyone sees it that way. I know who and what I AM.

How wonderful would our world be if our proclaimed peacekeepers/warmongers stopped the dick-measuring, drop all the egotistical threats, learn to feel both sides of the story, and cooperate!

Chapter 13

Acceptance

Acceptance comes in many forms. Letting go is difficult without awareness, appreciation and acceptance. Forgiveness does not come without a level of acceptance. To achieve complete freedom, we must appreciate, accept, forgive, and let go. Once you process acceptance and forgiveness, and then finally let go, you are giving yourself the gift of freedom.

Remember this "why bother"? Because: we all have something to forgive or be forgiven for.

On a low level and for the small things, "forgive and forget" is easy and has great value.

The thing is many of us are dealing with things that have been trivialized. But if we take a closer look, they are not so trivial. Letting go doesn't mean denial, burying or forgetting. Forgetting is simply not remembering. Forgiving and letting go are very closely related. Forgiveness does not have to contain forgetting when it can help someone else. Remembering doesn't mean that whatever the "it" is has to be or is constantly in your awareness. Forgiveness can have something tucked away in the memory bank without an emotional charge. That chapter of your story is finished, but it's still written down. Maybe it is permanently etched into your consciousness. Forgiveness contains the memory but is allowing your heart to be free even if it is scarred.

Lack of acceptance puts up a brick wall, closing off your heart and expresses an unwillingness to accept. Lack of acceptance comes from hate, anger, and disappointment—all elements of fear. All those bricks are a heavy burden. Acceptance will lighten the load.

How many of us are told to *just let go* or find forgiveness, but we can't? Maybe we can for a little while, but the challenge comes back and frustration sets in. That's because we are missing a step or two in the equation. There may be something lurking that is more than skin deep and may be "Crawling"- in your skin- *Linkin Park.* These wounds, they need to heal.

Picture in your mind what roots look like. Often, there is a tap root and then there are many other lateral roots that are meant to be supportive. Sometimes when you pluck something out by the roots and a piece of the main root remains, something can grow back. For us, emotional attachment grows back when support and acceptance are lacking. This is something to keep in mind if you start to beat yourself up over not letting go, so you can stop the self-flagellation and allow yourself to continue playing the role of the gardener. Take on the "I can" attitude. Go back. Observe. Try again.

Where is acceptance missing in your life? Where is support lacking? Where do you feel misunderstood? What have you not been able to let go of? What have you not forgiven? What continues to resurface? What makes you feel shackled and is preventing peace, harmony, and freedom?

Does it really matter? It's not all about you, right? Here comes the rub...*But it is all about you. You are what matters. In mastering your inner peace and freedom, you are mastering third dimension.*

If you are clear and have forgiven someone else, it doesn't matter if they haven't forgiven you. That's for them to come to terms with. You've done the best that you can.

THIS WAS A HUGE AWAKENING FOR ME! I trust that it will be for you, too.

When letting go, if you don't first embrace the emotion, the anger, the frustration, etc., as I have said before, and if you push emotion down, it will resurface and will rear its ugly head. If you keep it down, you will get sick in one form or another and keep the legal drug pushers in business as they suck you dry, and that legacy that you so desperately wanted to leave your children will disappear. What if you could leave them a whole new idea of legacy, including both inner and outer wealth in the crowning glory of peace?

Our emotions must come to the surface reaching a boiling point, so the steam can escape. Here is an example when keeping your mouth shut doesn't work, but neither does rehashing/reopening the same wound over and over, unless you are playing detective to solve a mystery. We have the ability and capability of communicating. We would all benefit from doing a better job of it. Pay attention to your role and responsibility in whatever transpired or is transpiring and be able to give your inner detective a description, not a label as on a pill bottle. Often once we have a description of a feeling; it is easier to let it go. If we are capable of describing it, then we are capable of understanding and accepting it. What prevents us from accepting is when we are stuck in "I don't know" or "I mean, you know" because you haven't faced or embraced whatever it is so we can reach that place.

Sometimes, in the idea of becoming conscious, we think we can just heal emotionally, and we don't need physical support; for example medical care, chiropractic care or medications. We have to honor both sides of the equation, and get whatever support we need. If you are lacking support, it means you need support. The idea is not to become overly dependent on support. Try some physical and emotional nurturing. See both sides of the equation; both sides of the story. Accept responsibility.

Stop expecting deep communication or understanding from people who aren't **presently** capable of either, and accept that whatever happened had happened for a reason. Also, accept that their emotional inability is not about you. That doesn't mean you can't say your peace, disengage from further attempts, or re-engage when you feel the time is right.

You are never too old, too young, too sick, or too busy to get this stuff. The "I'm toos" are excuses. Making an excuse is a choice, as well as an avoidance technique. Even if you don't feel quite ready to dive headfirst into healing, it is important to ask yourself; *what will it take for me to be ready.* There is no "I can" or "I will" when it comes to "I'm too." This is one technique that parents often use on kids. Then we, in turn, are often afraid to face our parents with things, because we think they are too old and will never "get it," or that it would be disrespectful, so they shouldn't be burdened. But the truth is we have been conditioned and manipulated into believing something that isn't necessarily true.

What is this really? It's a communication breakdown (*Led Zepplin,* "Communication Breakdown"). We learn until the day we die, and most likely beyond. There is continuous flow. This is Samsara. We agreed to incarnate with certain people. So shouldn't we honor that contract and support our human transformation? Even if we have circumstances that we avoid, because we know it would be toxic to our soul, doesn't mean that's what we can avoid ourselves. If Jesus really died to end our suffering, shouldn't we honor him by ending our own suffering, rather than perpetuating it and staying stuck in the past where we relive the horror? Acceptance is a key.

To the opposite side, we often don't give our kids enough credit by saying that they are "too young," "too immature," or "not ready." Through the eyes of innocence and without deep-conditioned beliefs, children can see more clearly. And if we pay attention, they can help break our brainwashing. If this occurs, you've done a good job at minimalizing their programming. That's something to be grateful for.

Some attempts to communicate on an earthly basis may be futile, especially if dementia or Alzheimer's disease has set in. That makes a communication breakdown easier to accept. It's harder to accept unwillingness, but if we have consciousness with a detached ego, it makes it easier. When you work with consciousness, you can still connect and communicate in a higher way. "Higher" is an appropriate term here, because you will be connecting with a person of higher self, which has a higher vibratory rate.

Regardless of present physical condition, physical presence, willingness or unwillingness, working with someone else of higher self helps in bringing you to a place of acceptance and resolve. This may be the only place where you can engage in cooperation. The first time you try reaching someone's higher self occurs more easily when facilitated. Seek outside assistance from an energy worker if you choose to try this route. NLP (Neuro Linguistic Programming), while not necessarily touted as energy work, is a great companion since it helps to release what is locked in our unconscious mind. NLP employs a technique called grief resolution. You need the intellectual acceptance and the heart-centered acceptance to get this energy out of your body entirely. There are times, we are so enmeshed in a relationship that, it is difficult for us to detach long enough to do what we need to do on our own. Facilitation may help you get cleared before you attempt to work with connecting to another on your own. Just remember, once you reach a resolution, to turn that feeling of resolve and acceptance towards yourself.

It isn't important to be concerned with someone else "getting it," because of the fact, whether or not they "get it" on this plane of existence doesn't matter. What matters is that you "get it." There is a commonly accepted belief that the not okays, only exist in this dimension. If this is true then in a higher dimension, those who appear not to "get it" in third dimension, will "get it" in the higher dimension. Therefore, in the higher dimension, they would be capable of offering what you need to get or hear from them. By going to the higher self, you have planted a seed for them to "get it" at another time. What they get and when they get it is up to them. It's not your job to fix others. This is about you and your freedom. Doggone it! It's okay to make this about you and your healing, growth, and expansion into living in present-moment consciousness.

Congratulations! You are on the road to accepting and loving yourself. What a good "why bother"!

Forgiveness is your ability to forgive. When you forgive someone else, you must remember to forgive yourself, too. Without acceptance, your ability to forgive may be hindered. So learn to accept whatever happened in the past and find the acceptance of self.

I had a profound direct personal experience in working with someone on an energetic level. Thank you, Tracy, for your unconditional love, support, and assistance; so that I could offer unconditional love and support to the person I was connecting with and to myself.

Crap, here I go, sharing some of the story…damn stories that we aren't supposed to tell. Sarcasm here people. As the Joker would say: "Why so serious, son?" In this case, it's "daughter." Song time: "Daughter"- *Pearl Jam*.

I've talked about my dad a bit here. Truly, I am not bashing or blaming him. It wasn't all conflict. I have some really fond memories and high regard for his finer attributes. He was a smart man and a good man who influenced many lives in positive ways. He just didn't understand his ego. He was unable to handle the guilt of what happened to me, or express his true feelings to me, so his ego fired back at me with anger. Though he was unable to say "I love you," on this plane, I have a deeper knowing that the love between us does exist. I understand that much of what occurred was just part of the contract.

So, it was way past time for my dad to let go and cross over. I don't say that to be cruel; it was a fact. I've already experienced the ego-emotional-based, attachment-based backlash from that comment. Growing up, I always heard him say that he would be dead by sixty, and at eighty-six and more health problems than in his words, "Carter's has liver pills," it was time for him to let go. It was just a simple fact that the body had given out.

A couple of years prior, being tired of all the b.s. that transpired and the things that didn't transpire that should have transpired, during an annual obligatory visit, I told him I was tired of disagreeing with him. And I said; "If I am so wrong about everything in life, come tell me when you cross over. I'll listen." I have had visits from ancestors, so I have experience in connecting with the other side.

That's not something, he ever talked about. I saw an element of belief in his eyes, and my request was met with a stare of challenge: "You're on."

This man swore he didn't want to live in pain; he didn't want to live if he couldn't really live his life. I recall an earlier time when he said, "This isn't living." Towards the end, he found himself in a state of needing constant attention in many ways. I knew there was a great deal of fear causing him to cling to existence for, clearly, life was no longer an option. Interesting were the words of denial by those who surrounded him: "The doctors are doing this or that so that he can have a better quality of life." All I could think was *in whose opinion of quality.*

Funny thing is, as toxic as my family was to me, in some way I was also toxic to them. After I left and my dad became physically weaker, he allowed himself to be more vulnerable. He started to express love and occasionally used the word "love." So I am told. While it was quite beautiful that the expression of love came forth regardless of how late, I could still see the element of fear. From my heart, I can say I am glad others got to experience his vulnerable side, knowing we can find strength in vulnerability.

Putting to practice what I had learned about working with the higher self, my intent was to help him to let go of some of those fears and allow him to see that there was absolutely no reason to fear whatsoever. There was not even a consideration that I would heal in the process. Duh! Anyone who has worked with energy knows what I am talking about.

In the connectedness, we are never truly disconnected. To feel the reconnection, we simply have to tap in. My friend, Tracy facilitated working on him once before. The first time, I felt an outside resistance. Though I had an idea of the source, I am not certain. In my experience, the divine realm always finds a way to reveal what it wants me to know. As validation, I received not one but two phone calls, and, in those conversations, it was revealed that he asked if I had been in his hospital room. Of course, he was chided for suggesting such a thing. Certainly, he knew I was 2400 miles away in Arizona. They thought he was hallucinating, and I kept my mouth shut like a good little girl. That was a clear revelation to me. As we become closer to physical death, the veil between worlds thins so part of him was willing to connect but not fully.

This second attempt to connect was different. As I focused on my breath, Tracy guided me to push energy through my body until the connection was reached. The energy was not met with resistance, but an amazing sense of love permeated the room. All of a sudden, for me, the energy changed and an issue bubbled to the surface inside of me. I did not express this to Tracy. What was coming up was the time when my dad said to me, *"You can go to any college you want, but it's a waste of money. You'll just get married and pregnant like your sisters."* As a teen, I perceived that as having no value. I won't second guess if I would have felt the same had I not been hiding the secret of my sexual abuse. Although I see now that it was my ego stepping in when those words were spoken to me about being a waste, I thought, *Why would anyone ever bring a child into this painful world? I am never having a child.*

In the energy process, I thought, *What the hell!*—as my ego, was simply trying to get my attention. *I thought I already let go of the worthy/unworthy bullshit.* Again, my ego tugged at present moment. My thought went to, *I am not trying to work on releasing my crap; I am trying to help him.* Once I let go of trying, I turned to my heart, focused my breath, and asked, *Why is this coming up, what do I need to see?* Looking for the good, I thought, *he gave me one of my most precious gifts, a gift that brought me joy*—my horses. *How could he tell me that I have no value?* I thought, *Come on, you've been through this before. You know it's all about control and perception. Just let it go.* The adult me "should be" able to intellectually and spiritually digest that, as I turned my attention to my root chakra and breathed.

Just then, Tracy said, "He's really sorry, Martha. He's sorry for everything."

I didn't tell her what I was processing; that came through her intuitively and authentically. You could dismiss this by saying, "Who wouldn't want their dad to say "I'm sorry" for something. After all, we all have something to forgive and be forgiven for."

But I've had too many experiences with energy to dismiss this. He brought up the issue, not me. Why? It had value to me. An aura of peace washed over me. Tracy exclaimed, "Wow! Martha, do you feel that?" Yep, I felt it.

Acceptance was automatic. With acceptance, forgiveness was not even necessary—because in the acceptance, there was nothing to forgive. It was an energy I chose to stay with for a while.

The call came the next morning, saying he had passed. It was within hours of doing this work on releasing fear and forgiveness. The physical suffering finally ended. Coincidence or synchronicity? While I recognize that my mother also told him it was okay to let go, which is of even greater value because of their connectedness, I believe the energy session impacted her as well, by allowing her to let go of her fear, and providing the courage to tell him it was okay. The energetic work we did should not be dismissed.

The divine realms that participate with us when we consciously choose to participate with them honor us the way that we honor them. We can share great power with their divinity. That divinity affects all of us and is recognized in the cosmos.

I can't talk about my dad without memories of our horses. My most precious experiences came from riding, and mostly riding with my dad. In those moments there was acceptance, nothing else mattered but being in nature and being free. There was a lot of control and conditions surrounding my relationship with my father making his love for me feel conditional. Memory flash: he always used the expression "them's conditions" to dismiss something. I recognize much extreme in the lessons and gifts but, also recognize that I chose to experience a full spectrum.

My first horse taught me about cooperation, unison, connection, and freedom. My second horse added an element on how to break the shackles of unconscious control. She was beautiful and spirited but very confused by me and my dad's opposing views of training. I took the whispering approach. My dad, used the old cowboy way with clenched fist and aggressive intimidation. Poor baby—she was so confused. I didn't want to abandon her. It was the only way I could set her and myself free. We rode in harmony, but she could never be completely controlled or broken, and neither can I.

See how this resonates for you; *Fireflight* – "Stand Up".

Chapter 14

Dysfunction

With all the talk of dysfunction that surrounds us, it would appear that dysfunction is more prevalent than function. So my question is: Why wouldn't we do everything in our power to change that? Consciousness changes what we don't know to what we do know. Consciousness changes dysfunction to function. "Conjunction Junction, what's your function?"—(*School House Rock*). It's up to each of us to find the conjunction, in our life spectrum, and choose to play on the side of function.

Earlier I said, we are over-intellectualizing and over-thinking spirituality, then I took it back and said or maybe under-thinking or not thinking at all. Regardless, the number one creator of problems in our world is abuse—abuse of every kind and atrocities against humanity. Every society on this planet suffers from abuse and dysfunction in some way and has since the human experience began. It's up to us to change it. It's up to us to end it.

We could start by learning how to communicate better. Too often, attention is placed on fault, blame, and guilt when we could be more focused on correcting behaviors. It would serve society, if we, broken adults, would take whatever happened to us, and transform that into better relationships and interactions by exercising consideration, which requires both thought and feeling.

If our children are our future, let's start with them. If you have squashed a child in some way, through misguided interaction, step up, be the adult, be the bigger person and apologize *sincerely*. Don't be afraid to let them know that our entire life is a learning process, and that you are still figuring things out. Thank them for helping you see your flaws so you can be a better parent or person. Letting go of your wounds for their sake and acknowledging their feelings does not dismiss yours. Get out of your ego and accept your responsibility in the story.

When we look at bad behavior, it would be wise to pay attention to the way we express words. A kid being a kid does not make a bad kid. For example; if a kid makes a mess, it may be an inconvenience for an adult but the mess is not usually made maliciously, yet, how often does a supposed adult freak out. The way we speak to kids is why we have so many adults who don't know how to take personal responsibility or know how to hold themselves accountable. Instead, we have the "I didn't do it" or "It's not my fault" syndrome or adults who are clueless to their inappropriate reactions.

We hear a lot of parents say, "I give up," "I can't take it anymore" and "I've tried everything." Are you sure? There are times when it's our lesson to back off and let go. Other times our kids are crying out for help and don't know how to communicate what they need. Parents need to get out of their ego, tap into awareness and look at how their own dysfunctional upbringing could be creating this. If we really want to help our children, maybe we should save ourselves? (*Stabbing Westward*—"Save Yourself") A kind, caring, adult will periodically check in to see if everything is okay, without being overbearing. There are bound to be challenges, but at least you know you are doing your best to show love.

Adults like to say, "That's just how it is," "That's how it's always been" or "That's how I was raised." That doesn't make it right. If you excuse dysfunction because you had a dysfunctional background, or if you label yourself as dysfunctional, you will be dysfunctional. Dysfunction and abuse are not okay.

With a slight twinge of envy for those who have come from spiritually and emotionally supportive upbringings, I also have a deep appreciation for it. In feeling that I did not have the experience of support, I recognize and accept this is a path I chose for this incarnation. It's given me an opportunity to really look at just how dysfunctional we are on this planet.

Practicing consciousness has shown me, as it can show you, that we can create functional relationships. If we allow it, life's equal and opposite reactions bounce us back as far out as we have gone in any direction. The ability to bounce back, emotional resilience, is saving yourself.

"Holding on to anger is like drinking poison and expecting the other person to die."—Source unknown

*"I have forgiven everyone in my story. If they haven't forgiven me, it's not my problem."—*I don't know who said this. Right now, it's *Me.*

"It isn't always what a person does that is painful, or counts, for that matter. Sometimes what they don't do is just as painful and just as valuable."—Me

Even in writing this book, resistance to having my voice heard surfaced because my parents were unintentionally clueless to the words they spoke. My dad's words; *Keep your mouth shut and keep the peace* and, *there's not a goddamn thing wrong with you that a good crack in the ass won't fix.* Mom's words; *What makes you think you are so special.* And more. Many lessons come in the form of dreams. If we are open and paying attention, they will often disturb us with a metaphoric wake-up call. So here is my dream— wake-up call:

A woman offered to give me a massage while I was getting my haircut. Suddenly, while being massaged, I am suffocating, and my head is underwater with her hands covering my mouth. There was a lucid curiosity without fear, that it didn't feel like I was drowning but suffocating. *Struggling against her, I pulled myself up out of the sink and said, "I can't do this with my head underwater."* It was a simple

137

matter of fact statement. When we become more conscious, we become more matter of fact.

She muttered something in annoyance, but we moved to a regular table, and the massage continued. Next thing I know, her hands are over my mouth again. This time, I really had to struggle and fight to break free and take a breath. Whew! Refusing to allow her to continue, she was quite offended and even said, "<u>That's the way we do it here</u>." Ya think that represented conditioning like the *Shirley Jackson* story I mentioned earlier and a clear message that some things are no longer acceptable? I can't help but laugh at the obvious messages in this dream, both clear and metaphoric since it parallels how I felt about my family's reaction to my exposing my sexual abuse.

In my 30s, the issue had been bubbling below the surface. My soul decided it was time to pull the trigger on a wake-up pistol. After being robbed at gunpoint, a total stranger expressed more concern for my well-being than my ex-husband. Soon after that my healing adventure was locked and loaded. I don't need coddling, but a simple "Are you okay?" or an "Anything I can do," would have been nice. I resisted bringing up the ex at all in this book. However, I will digress to a lower form of myself to admit that I refer to the ex as *"he-who-shall-not-be-named."* It's my way of not giving my energy away. Is that unkind? It's a metaphoric joke, people, and a small price to pay for what I was put through. So bitch slap me if you like, I need something to make me laugh about a sucky part of my life. I also recognize that Gollum didn't start out as Gollum and there is still good in him. Whhaat? He used to do a good Gollum impersonation. Anyway, sometime after the robbery, I confronted *him* about his lack of concern for my well-being. His response was, "Part of me hoped you had died, so I could collect your life-insurance money." Wow! I attracted exactly what I was conditioned to attract; lack of support or compassion. This triggered the suppressed memories to bubble just above the surface where before they had bubbled just below. Of course, he also told me that *if I ever left him, that I would die alone because everyone hated me.* Now, I can say, "oh okay, that was cruel" without emotion, but before

I began to heal from sexual abuse, part of me believed it. Now can you see why I didn't want to give him any energy?

How many of us resist telling our story out of fear, out of shame, out of guilt, or out of feeling like we are small and unimportant?

My soul created disturbances to wake me up and bring issues out of denial and above the surface, so I could let my soul be my pilot.

How many of us remain in "Resistance" (*Muse*) when what we really need is an "Uprising" (*Muse*).

Today, we need "uprisings" in many areas. Dysfunction and abuse are rampant. Both need to be brought to the surface, rather than deny their existence. This is an area where the ego needs to be held accountable for all the complaining and blaming. It needs to be shut up and let authenticity propel us into motion. Something got lost in translation about the sin of denying our maker (God). Maybe it was about the sin of denying what we have made; a world full of abuse. Maybe the real sin is the denial of the god that is in each of us. Being abusive denies God. (There's *Alice In Chains*, again)

My story of abuse is not meant to cause any story-participants pain, rather it is intended to create awareness. In the words of Spock, "The needs of the many outweigh the needs of the few." Knowing how prevalent sexual abuse is in our society, how it affected me, and how consciousness shifted my perception and initiated healing on every level of my being and soul, the beings of light in other realms have let me know that I have a responsibility to tell my story.

Often people only do what they are taught and conditioned to do. By accepting what is not acceptable, the ego takes over in protective mode. This doesn't place fault nor does it usurp responsibility to change. Things happen in our lives that stop emotional growth. This is why we have so many adults who don't/can't/won't express in an adult way. We may never know why some go through life unable to see their own dysfunction, let alone step beyond it. But, there are plenty of us who want to make a change. For me, in changing dysfunction to function, I have developed momma bear instincts (more likely wolverine) without sheltering or coddling my daughter and myself. I recognize that my mother's emotion growth was choked off before she could develop those instincts, and I accept that. She was kind in her idea of kind; a good caretaker. But, poor me, I ended up marrying someone emotionally choked-off like her! Oh the scars! Kidding! "I'm Free"-*The Who*.

Very simply, I AM, no longer a victim. To say that I have never caused someone pain would be a lie. It would be nearly impossible to go through an entire life without hurting someone else in some way, even with the best intentions not to. With a conscious intent set on breaking karma and never stepping into the role of the victimizer, we have better odds. That is living in integrity to the best of our ability.

As a deeper part of my story is revealed (*Led Zeppelin,* "Kashmir"), it is my sincere desire that the reveal provides something to help you see that our stories can be changed from maniacal to magical. It is only because I said **NO** to abuse and dysfunction that I have become a magician, and we all can. "Abracadabra"– (possibly Aramaic –"I create what I speak" – also a song by *Steve Miller*)

The many that I wish to inspire are the one in five females and the one in six males who are, or once were, victims of sexual abuse. Staggering! Those numbers are just what have been reported. Those numbers must be much greater, as there are many others, like me, whose abuse was never reported. Let's include all who have suffered from any kind of abuse and the antihero who also needs healing, love and forgiveness. That's a lot of people. No wonder our world is mad.

Making a play of our inward journey facilitates healing through appreciation, acceptance, forgiveness, freedom and peace so we can all step beyond just coping with the past.

My family says that I like to argue. You can't debate with people who are always right and unaware of childish-ego. The fact is that I despise arguing, and it causes me great distress. It's interesting that when you present some people with truth, and they are unable to dispute the truth, in their wanting to deny the truth, that their ego perceives this as argumentative when the truth is that they are just uncomfortable with the discussion. It's hard for me to know that I am seen this way when my only intent is to create conscious response to an ugly topic. Justice and fairness tug at my heartstrings even when that creates a tug of war. It's a fairly safe bet that many of you have experienced a conversation being shut down through accusation. I've been accused of being the troublemaker when my attempt is to implement positive change. Suggesting that the whole family, including myself was dysfunctional was shunned with an attitude of, "I know you are but what am I."

I know I am not alone as I listen to and read the lyrics of the song by *Fireflight,* "Unbreakable." I can't be broken, broken is an illusion. If you've ever been "the bad man," follow *Fireflight* with *The Who's* "Behind Blue Eyes."

Damn, I must still have some Marthyr, I mean martyr program running. How could I be the bad man when I was the one being abused? Only one member of my immediate family ever voluntarily validated me by saying what happened was wrong. The rest turned more than just a blind eye. They turned their back. It would appear supportive if someone said, "I don't' know how I can help but, if there is anything I can do, please don't hesitate to ask." No family member said that. Those words would have been supportive, functional and appropriate to someone you love. But, I wasn't dealing with real adults, just adult bodies. As I began to search for ways to heal, strangers would say, "I'm sorry that happened to you." Like the song, "Unbreakable" says "Where are the people that accused me?"…."Can't face me in the light." Even a blind person can sense light and dark. A turned back leaves you with an empty out-stretched hand. Let it go. Move on. That isn't about you. Love them from a distance even if you crave intimacy.

In all fairness, that is not entirely true. My biological family could face me, so long as they did not have to deal with or attempt to understand what happens to a person when they experience the trauma of sexual abuse. In fact, I was asked—no, reverse that. The statement was made: "If you buried it all these years, why would you bring it up now?" It was a statement expressed with the kind of anger that shuts you down. How dare I upset everyone else? "Damn it, why can't you just keep your mouth shut; always causing trouble." Is it any wonder I suppressed the memories of my youth? Attempts to communicate the reason for my silence just did not go through. The blue pill blocked it.

It's okay. I embrace them, even if they can't, won't or don't embrace me, because I know, that this version of reality is an illusion controlled by ego. I know that in the dimension where Christed-consciousness exists, the not okay's are non-existent. Therefore, in the higher dimensions of reality, their egos would respond differently. But, I must be honest; I was hurt and pissed. I felt angry and betrayed, and I felt guilty for having hate in my heart. Hate was very hard to embrace because I don't even like the word let alone want it in me. Embracing it through Heart-Centered Conscious Knowing, is the only way, that I could integrate and transform that kind of emotion into compassion.

I observed another family situation when a secret was kept. That situation when revealed was met with ire. I wasn't mad. I felt bad that she obviously couldn't trust me either. When I piped up in her defense and asked, "Has anyone considered what made her feel like she couldn't trust anyone enough to be forthcoming," I was told, "it's none of your business." Once again, I was under the mistaken impression that when a family member was in some sort of obvious pain that it was family business to try to help and protect. No, I was not mistaken. Family is supposed to show love and support? Thank you for showing me the truth.

My heart does not allow me to feel resentment towards my immediate family, only sadness. I often wonder where the coldness began. I wonder how they react when they see stories of abuse; like the Penn State sexual abuse case, or the story of a father who killed his daughter's molester, and let's not forget the rampant abuse by Catholic priests. Have they considered how they would have felt if it had been them or my nieces or nephews? Do they know pedophiles are jailed? Is it terrible? Is it as terrible as the weather and the traffic? They seem to be capable of expressing emotion about gas, groceries and coupons? Has my abuse and how it affected me ever cross their mind? I wonder how they would have reacted, had it been anyone other than me. All that matters now is that my story has the ability to help others.

I would not have known the depth of the dysfunction without the transformational powers heart-centered conscious knowing provides. Dysfunction didn't start with me, but I wasn't going to continue to play nice because others had warped perception of what that means.

If you have suppressed or repressed emotions and have been abused, I encourage you to become conscious. Go to your heart, higher self, intuition, and let it tell you what it knows about the circumstance that you faced. Let your free will change the outcome by starting with something to appreciate even if that appreciation at first seems small and unrelated or start by exploring what *not appreciating* feels like. Most likely you won't want to hold on to that.

I have never read a book or participated in a support group, specifically on sexual abuse. In no way am I knocking support groups, and they may be a good place for you to start. After all, it's called support for a reason. My heart just didn't feel like it was important for me to take that path and besides that I was conditioned not to seek support. Early on, I would have dismissed anything with the word "support" in the title. Conscious knowing doesn't erase the not okay's, it helps you to see the truth of it.

Knowing that someone else has had it worse is not an excuse to dismiss your pain or deny yourself from getting help. Use your knowing to help support others and heal yourself in the process. Synchronicity sparked memories from the past as I was writing. Memories that no longer arose like a pulled trigger, evidencing that I had let go. What remains is sparked passion; a passion to express and help others to find courage in their own voice.

Synchronicity also prompted me to do a little research. Since *unworthy* and *abandon* have changed to *accepted* and *supported*, it is easier to let go but it doesn't mean you can't call for back-up.

The following is from the Arizona Center for Change; Diane Genco, MA, LPC:

There are many forms of sexual abuse. These include: childhood sexual abuse by an adult, sexual assault/rape, date rape, being manipulated into sex, sibling sexual abuse, etc. Sexual abuse can occur in a "hands off" way as well. "Hands off" abuse can include being shown pornography at a very young age, a person exposing themselves to you, or a person "peeping" in on you when you did not want them to. "Hands on" abuse includes contact where the abuser made direct sexual contact with you or forced you to have contact with another person. <u>Regardless of the kind of abuse you experienced, the effects can be traumatizing and create lifelong patterns of "victim like" behavior for the victim.</u>

Emotional: Sexual abuse can have significant effects on a person's ability to experience and regulate emotions. *Some victims are very detached from emotions while others experience emotions in a very deep and overly sensitive manner.*

Knowing that the above is true, how could anyone, be expected, to stay in relationships that lack support, consideration or sensitivity towards your experience? For me, the traumatic events are over. My choice to disengage from family did not stem from the acts. At the core of my choice to disengage was the dismissal of my feelings. Not only were there multiple acts of abuse by multiple abusers, there were multiple toxic relationships that required healing. Relationships can't heal from just one side. They must heal in both directions. If that isn't happening trim the root and keep your distance until you are stronger.

Toxin was flying at me from multiple aspects of environment. You know the saying, "What doesn't kill you makes you stronger"? Beauty was there too, but I literally believed the toxic side was going to kill me. With newfound support, my choosing to leave was met with resistance by those who fed like vampires on my strength, but my soul was determined to detox.

Learning to forgive my predators didn't mean that the events never happened, nor does it excuse what happened. While I sympathize with the second victimizer, and the fact that he was abused as a child too, that does not make what happened, acceptable. I only hope that he finds peace. The first abuser just doesn't matter, because my family's lack of support overshadowed any feelings I had about him. Though, I do remember how it all started with him. Tickling is supposed to be fun, but is considered abusive when the tickler won't stop. It should never turn into molestation. It's sad when you try to tell, but are shut down, and told, "you asked for it" before you can get the words out. It took a lot of fun and playfulness out of my life. Drug abuse came into the mix, in many ways, but that's a dimension that serves no purpose right now. As you listen, please also read the lyrics to the song "Broken Girl" by *Matthew West.*

When abuse is picked up by a second man, you question whether or not you really did ask for it. You are a kid, how do you know how to handle adult things? I don't blame my parents. Like I said before, sometimes you just don't know what you just don't know. You would assume when your father consistently tells you to use your head, that he was using his. Obviously, he didn't use his head to think about how his words would mess me up. This is not judgment. It's just the truth. He would clench his fist and raise his voice at the mention of anything emotional. His ego overshadowed anyone's need. I misperceived any need of mine, as being a cry baby. The church and my mom's religious convictions made the cry baby think she had a devil inside of her. I was bitten by a dog that didn't cause me to be frightened of dogs. I was robbed at gun point that didn't cause me to stay in fear or to be afraid of guns. Words, molestation, sexual abuse, that caused emotional terror– "Hell Is For Children"– *Pat Benatar.*

Healing takes time. A physical illness or injury is often easier for others to accept. Emotional injury is not as easily accepted. For many years, I tolerated and coped with living in dysfunction but it was no longer acceptable. If you have suffered, find strength in the suffering and channel it into making you stronger.

Voices (*Alice in Chains*- "Voices") in my head from before, during, and after my abuse began:

Words of others: "That mouth's going to get you in trouble." "Keep your mouth shut and keep the peace." When I begged to go to counseling, "There's not a goddamn thing wrong with you that a good crack in that ass won't fix." "You don't know what problems are." Those words twisted my mind and twisted like a blade in my heart. More than once I was judged for seeking help and made to feel I was not deserving of it. Ignorance leads victims to believe it's their own fault. Add to that; "You asked for it." "You're just a brat." "Settle down."

Word of others mixed with my own self-imposed words of torture: *They get angry when you stand up to them. There's that clenched fist and the "So help me God." God? I'm scared what God will do to me. The church says we are all sinners. God must be punishing me. They know more than me. No one likes a tattle-tale. Emotions are weak, be strong. Forget it. After all, they've all been through so much worse than you. You know the war and the Great Depression; they were really poor, and they were poor when the older kids were born. You're so ungrateful. You have no idea what that's like. That matters more than being held down and fondled or having a dick stuck in your face while you sleep—and don't say that word; it's dirty. It has to be your fault. You must have asked for it; otherwise, it wouldn't have happened in the first place. And they both did it. Is this really how men are? You're expected to be a good Catholic girl. Certainly, what happened to you is nothing compared to what they've been through. You're the brat who gets everything. How are you going to get to heaven unless you suffer? Jesus suffered, why shouldn't you? And they have sacrificed, so you can have that horse. They already said, if you cause trouble, they will take it away. They always say that I am ridiculous. You can't bother them with ridiculous problems. You must have asked for it prancing around in shorts. And wearing a two-piece bathing suit? You should be covered up; it wouldn't have happened if you have been covered up. Slut! No wonder no one loves you. I'm confused; other girls wear a two piece. You're so stupid. They have enough to deal with without dealing with you, you ungrateful piece of shit? And you were told to keep your mouth shut and keep the peace. Peace? The only way to keep peace is not to tell. The only way I can find peace with all this chatter in my head is to shove it down so they don't shove that fist down your throat that they are always threatening to do. God I hate myself, it's no wonder everyone else hates me too.*

Sound ridiculous. It's not! Pretend it never happened. This is what abuse victims of all sorts go through. Rather than play the tape over and over, you bury it. Your ego allows it to resurface when it wants to protect you; your authentic-self replays it when it wants to motivate you to heal. Don't wrong the ego. It serves a purpose. My ego was my champion until my authentic self was strong enough to break free. Much of what crippled my healing along my journey was the misperception that my ego was bad! I didn't know I needed to learn to EMBRACE and ACCEPT all aspects of me before I could learn to love.

Get support. I only knew the word "support" in the support hose my mom wore. Now that I see the connection between physical pain and emotional pain, I see that somewhere in my mother's life, she perceived herself as not being supported. We can't expect support from those who do not know how give or offer it. Instead, we can learn to be supportive. That doesn't mean others will take you up on the offer.

In my family, sarcasm prevailed and everything bad that happened to someone else was a joke. Doing mean things to other people was funny. Teasing was usually more of a personal attack. If you didn't like it, you were warned with an iron fist, "You better learn to take it" or "You better get a thicker skin." The dysfunctional history of this was made really obvious to me when a toddler in the family was just learning to walk, fell and my mom said, "Ha-ha, the devil knocked you down." I thought my head was going to spin around like *Regan MacNeil* ("The Exorcist"). Then she said, "that's what my mother used to say." The comment was completely unconscious. Consciously, that's a pretty sick thing to say to a toddler, but a good example of how programmed dysfunction begins. No one else even noticed the words or gave it a passing thought. Our words have vibration, and these words were not of magical vibration.

Here's a quote I pilfered from the Internet that is not credited to anyone in particular. Again, it must be true because it was on the Internet:

> There's always a little truth behind every, "Just kidding." A little curiosity behind every, "Just wondering." A little knowledge behind every, "I don't know." A little emotion behind every, "I don't care." And a little pain behind every "I'm okay."

Joking or teasing is fun when you get it from someone who also gives the opposite of love and support. When you can laugh at yourself *with* someone who supports you, it is an entirely different dynamic and energy than when ribbing, poking and jabbing come in the form or mockery. I was often told that I had no sense of humor. False! Not true. It's just that without support, the rib poking is venomous. The ribbing is the venom; love and support is the antidote.

This also from the Arizona Center for Change Web site; Diane Genco, MA, LPC:

EMOTIONAL SUPPORT:

We strongly encourage you to identify a "wheel of support." You should begin talking to people in your support system and telling them of your decision to begin your journey of recovery. This will be helpful because there might be a time down the road that you will need to call on them for something related to your treatment. Informing them beforehand will help tremendously.

My plea for help as an adult was simply disregarded, the same as when I was a kid, begging to see a counselor. My earthly biological parents saw that as ridiculous and I was continually told how my feelings were wrong. Yes, Caroline Myss, I was born to the wrong tribe or not.

Ignorance is a lack of knowledge. It doesn't mean that they intended to be. Ignorance to me is not bliss. Their fear, denial, ego, and emotion over-shadowed my pain. The prevailing attitude, my biological family, took towards the revelation of facts was embarrassment. "Martha, you are embarrassing yourself." What that really meant was, "You are embarrassing us." I was told to settle down about my abuse while they got their dander up over junk mail and telemarketing in their next breath.

As a kid, I attempted suicide once. I lay in bed for two days from a failed overdose. My mom thought I had the flu. My other-worldly family made sure that I was staying. Admittedly they had a challenge keeping me here. Had it not been for my one "Avalon Sister" (*Cyndi Lauper*), I would have completely run away, and not had the opportunity to practice being an observer. She heard my cry even amidst her own suffering in quietude.

Here is a much lighter story to see the value of the observer as I experienced it. When I was about three, I hated green beans. But they were my dad's favorite. I didn't like anything about them: the taste, the texture, the smell. Yuk! My parents were determined to force me to eat them but I was NOT giving in. As forcefully as the beans were shoved into my mouth, they exploded just as forcefully out of my body with the rest of my meal all over my plate and the rest of the table. They weren't peas but they were still green and this was before *The Exorcist*. Turns out, I may have been the original devil child.

Trust me. I don't take the story part seriously! Who doesn't have some sort of story about their parents' attempt to impose force? Who doesn't get a good laugh at someone puking? But there is a setup and a reference point here so stay with me. Also contained here is metaphor for being force-fed outdated beliefs.

149

During a pilgrimage home, almost fifty years after the bean incident, one said to another, "You brought green beans. Martha doesn't eat green beans." I tightened my forehead, looked up a little to search my memory and thought, *Hmm...that was really interesting.* It may have been, or should I say, "bean" well intentioned; but it brought up some major realizations for me. How could I expect them to see me as I am now when they are not capable of seeing me as the teen who was sexually abused and can only see me as the three-year-old, devil child, who threw up green beans all over the kitchen table?

Talk about not letting go and being stuck in the past. It's actually quite amusing when you come up with these "aha's." The mirror technique took on a whole new glow. They were right; I did ask for it, and it is my fault! Often when traumatized, we get stuck at the point of traumatization. I traumatized them when I was three, so they couldn't see me beyond that. Granted, in a normal situation, this story would be stupid, but what is stupid, when stupid shows you dysfunction, and creates a new perception which brings comfort. And, by the way, I don't hate green beans; I just dislike my mom's green beans.

As a teen, I lived on antacids until I moved out. Why? Because; I could not digest the verbal toxin that I was being fed, and it was my body's way of dealing with the stress brought on by what was happening. Along with that, I was unable to trust anyone with anything. Our bodies communicate with us if we listen. Indigestion disappeared after I moved out.

When I came clean about what happened, hoping to get support, I admit that I had held it in for so long that it was not just bubbles coming to the surface—it was a volcano erupting like the day I puked up the beans so I finally got some counseling. After a couple of sessions, the counselor said, "I owe you an apology."

I said, "Wait, what? An apology? To me? Why is that?"

He said, "The first time I talked to you, I thought you might be delusional. I see now that you have been holding this in for a long time, and you've never been <u>validated</u>." My counselor felt it important to

<u>further validate</u> me by sharing that he spoke to my medical doctor who had a much higher opinion of me than I had of myself. Remember what I said in Chapter 3 under expectations? I had no concept of validation beyond a parking ticket. People have always seen me as strong but on the inside I was in pain. It's been said that you only need validation from yourself, but I really benefited from the support validation provided. While still not from my family, suddenly, validation appeared all around me. So now for some feel-good spontaneity: *Police,* "Synchronicity I or II"? Definitely both. Oooh...Oooh...Oooh.

The right counselor provided a great deal of help in only a few sessions. I had *never* experienced compassion of the magnitude he expressed. I needed a break from the intensity of what I released, but recovery was not complete. Being around toxic family making ignorant comments, triggered more volcanic fissures.

My mother's words would echo: "There's nothing we could have done because of how you were."

What could that even mean? What kind of response is that? Is this one of those I mean, you knows when someone doesn't know?

Those of us who have taken the red pill must remember that those who took the blue pill don't even remember taking it.

So if someone you would have hoped would express concern for you, can't, won't or doesn't, nurture yourself.

Me: "But I'm telling you now."
Mom: "Well, I don't know what you *expect* me to do about it now."

She was really good being ego-defensive, and making it about her. She didn't play much offense; in fact, she didn't play much at all. Strangers and true friends have said, *what happened to you is wrong, I'm sorry you had to go through that.* At what was supposed to be home, there was only disappointment, insensitivity and ridicule for reading self-help books. I didn't have great expectations, but I also didn't expect to have what happened to me, be trivialized. I don't know what you *expect me to say* is different than *I don't know what to say*. Not only did I have to lower my expectations, I had to let go of them all together. *All I'm askin' is for a little respect.* What generation doesn't love *Aretha Franklin's- "Respect?"* Respect works both ways. Wanting to heal is not disrespectful. Not healing is disrespectful to God and god.

Even I didn't realize that I had a mild form of PTSD; where one word can fire you off and my family had no consideration for this. Knocking me off balance was funny and intentional. In a way, it was as inconsiderate as setting a bottle down in front of an alcoholic. Their interactions with one another don't require the same consideration. I am simply a reminder of something that makes them uncomfortable; a dirty little secret. This may sound sick but there is a part of me that is proud to be their "Dirty Little Secret" – *All American Rejects. Why?* Because; I know the truth and I can celebrate it.

I repeat this with purpose. "Go where you are celebrated, not where you are tolerated."—Unknown

I am sure there are those who will think the words that I have expressed about my mother are unkind. What they may or may not realize, or may or may not actually hear, is that this is not about judgment or blame, but simply about my experience. I have seen parents cry and families support a victim, but also know those whose experience lacked support. So while the experience of abuse varies and while mine may not have been as severe, all abuse victims need some kindness and compassion. How can anything ever change without this awareness?

I recognize, others have experienced a kinder, gentler side of my mother. If their egos feel a need to protect her, that's probably good for her. If what I have to say disturbs someone, then I would hope that it would disturb them enough to discover the truth of their own disturbances. When and if they hear this and think that I have not let go, I hope it disturbs them into looking at what it is they need to let go of. Letting go doesn't dismiss the facts.

When I first talked about the abuse, I didn't even recognize it as abuse. Janie, who this book is dedicated to, came to my rescue, and she wasn't wearing a superhero costume. She was authentic. She took me through some dark processing, most of which I don't even remember anymore evidencing that I have let go. She was the first person I ever trusted enough to tell my tale of woe long before I came clean with my family. Her support provided me the courage to tell them and stand up for myself. I made that choice. She knew I wasn't seeking pity. I was seeking a way to end suffering.

Mom always criticized people for being selfish, criticized those who acknowledged their accomplishments and criticized people for criticizing. I thought it would be selfish and critical to expose the abuse while it was happening. That would make me a bitch and I didn't want that. When I was burying what happened, I was protecting everyone around me. I was afraid that if I told my dad, he might kill someone and go to jail. The family would lose him, and I would be to blame. I was afraid that if I told the villains' wives, I would be responsible for destroying marriages, and I would be responsible for tearing the family apart. There were small children who could get hurt.

Dysfunction prevailed in a mad world. I was protecting everyone around me. I was being *selfless*, while being accused of being selfish. There was no point in telling Mom, for fear she would wash my mouth out with soap for even saying the word "sex," and then drag me off to a priest, so they could tell me that I was dirty, and that I must confess *my* sins. Probably quiet lucky for me not to see a priest.

God punishes disobedience. I was being obedient to my dad's words: "Keep your mouth shut and keep the peace." By being obedient, maybe someone could love me. I felt shame, blame, guilt, and responsibility. If I were a good person, this wouldn't be happening to me, so I must be bad. I could get in trouble. I didn't want to ruin everything. Ruin was one of my mom's favorite words.

To do penance for my sins without confession, I must protect everyone else. I was shouldering this tremendous burden when I was hearing the words, "You know how she is; she's such a brat." Even now, I am seen as a selfish bitch, but I know it's because I won't tolerate or allow their unjust behavior. They still say "You know how she is," when they don't know a thing.

It is common for one to keep quiet about abusive trauma. It's common for the victimizer to tell the victim to keep quiet. It wasn't necessary in this case. My parents caused enough subconscious, subhuman damage for me to stay quiet and the rest of the family perpetuated that. Still, I could intellectually forgive that, but something was missing in my ability to completely forgive.

I know, when I first started to express, it was from a place of heightened sensitivity. I ADMIT, that I didn't always express kindly. I was filled with anger. I was venomous; I was toxic. Sarcasm was all I knew. For many years, I endured being in the same room with my attacker/s while hiding my pain, trying to keep the peace. I didn't have much of a reference point for expressing, let alone from a perspective of kindness, nor did I have the experience to deal with what was going on inside of me. For that, I AM sorry.

It's all good now. I accept not being accepted.

I've learned to become kinder and gentler, because expression through the heart allows a fulfilled knowing of truth and wisdom. Knowing that love fuels the flame of passion, all your problems will feel as if they were not watered down but washed away, creating a whole new clarity that has reaches an apex of peace.

Appreciation. Acceptance. Joy. Love. Fulfillment. Freedom. Peace.

Can you see all the words from the introduction of the book and how they fit into the seven chakra system and how they actuate healing? In Chapter 15, we are going to expand that to eleven for a full blown celebration of healing before we move on to "letting go" and "forgiveness".

None of this is just about my story. It's to give voice to all those who have been abused, in any way, who have not yet found theirs. It is meant to show you, not tell you, how waking up and consciousness can benefit everyone. You never really know a feeling until you experience it. Periodically run through the words and take notice to where each resonates for you. Give a little extra embrace to the ones that feel stuck. Life begins and ends with breath, so rebirth yourself with each breath until you reinvent or recreate what you want. Move at your own pace. Don't dwell, but don't let "just get over it", hinder you. In the know time, you are being presented with what you know.

It's all right now. (*Free, "All Right Now"*) This song was written by *Free* but what a great metaphoric joke, even if the timing is backwards that some members were part of *Bad Company*.

Chapter 15

Unconditional Love and the Heart Pillar Exercise

Let's forget about love or loving for this exercise. Not that love isn't important, it is; but when we have been wounded we have to find a path to love, beyond just the idea of love. Unconditional love is not the same as loving or being in love.

Eleven is considered by many to be of significance biblically, spiritually and a master number in numerology. I was given 11 words by my etheric high council, my support team, for us to work with which will guide us into seeing that we can find unconditional love in our hearts without the attachments that come with other forms of love.

This is an introduction to a technique called the Heart Pillar given to me by the same high council. With a little basic instruction and using the eleven words below, I invite you to play with this to gain a sense of what true unconditional love feels like. If judgment or any other feeling gets in your way, embrace it until you are able to sense the true meaning of the word you are working on. Remember that you may only get to a level of sense before you are able to connect with the actual feeling. Hopefully, this will encourage you to practice.

Remember to breathe fully, deeply, rhythmically. We will be creating a heart pattern in your energetic field that starts below your feet, comes up the front of your body; arcs and touches down into the base of your crown chakra, arcs again to create the top of the heart. We then send the energy down your back to finish the heart pattern.

We create a layering of hearts with each word, and each word begins at a different place in the body which you will find below. After each heart is created you will send energy down your body.

The purpose of going over your back is to help you start to think in 3-D. Do not connect the energy at the starting and stopping point of the heart. Simply allow the energy to blend.

The energy pillar is created by moving through each word in a different place of the body. Each breath is pulled up from below your feet, and you will start to focus on the word when the breath reaches the body part suggested below. Each body part is also the starting a stopping point of each heart. By pulling the energy up the body, the pillar is created. As you go over the back and through the body part where you started the heart, send the energy back down through the pillar. It's almost as if you are running up and down a xylophone. The hearts layer upon one another until you reach the crown. When you reach the crown, let it create a heart that starts at the "v" point of the layered hearts and create a heart that surrounds light that shines above the crown to connect with divine unconditional love. Allow this light to come back down through the crown, and run all the way through the pillar, through all the hearts in each chakra including the ones below your root, through your feet and into the earth. As you play with this, you can allow the newly created energy to spin, rotate and spiral.

Appreciation – Start and end with this beneath your feet. Let this be a foundation for everything.

Gratitude – Start and end at your ankles. Let this be support and stability.

Grace – Start and end at your knees. Let this be your ability to move graciously, fluidly and flexibly.

Acceptance – Start and end at your root chakra. Let this be a new root to accepting that whatever happened, has happened to show you truth even if what happened was an unacceptable situation.

Forgiveness – Start and end in your sacral chakra (belly). Let this be for you to fore give; to give yourself peace in advance of any stressful situation or memory, past, present, future.

Happiness – Start and end in your solar plexus. Let this be the smile that brightens even the darkest moments.

Peace – Start and end in your heart. Let this be permeable in every moment; permanently enabled.

Mercy – Start and end in your high heart. Let this be the bridge where the good and bad in everything is greeted with mercy. It is what it is; Isis. Let the goddess Isis be your guide.

Communication – Start and end in your throat. Let this be the ability to communicate with kindness, gentleness and compassion even in unharmonious conversations.

Vision – Start and end in your third eye. Let this be your ability to view the truth with a clear perspective.

Freedom – Start and end in your crown. Let this be your crowning glory of wisdom.

How did that feel? Did you start to sense unconditional love without labelling love? By not connecting the point at the bottom of the heart you allowng your heart to remain open and not creating a never ending cycle of karma. Unconditional love is what the idea of being heart-centered is about. Unconditional love allows third-dimensional pain to dissipate. The pillar creates a new sense of stability because you have created a connection to pure source while being grounded to the earth core.

Chapter 16

Forgiveness and Freedom

Another first—Janie gifted me with the audio version of the book by Caroline Myss, *Why People Don't Heal and How They Can*. It greatly benefited me to listen and listen more than once. Caroline Myss coined the term "woundology" that I referred to in Chapter 3 and it was her portrayal of how we are hurt by the people who love us the most that really got me *thinking* about how this could be true, and why, I would have created this whole sexual abuse mess, the trauma and the wounds, which put me on a long road of discovery and recovery, especially since now I was feeling guilty about creating it.

While it's not the same for everyone, for me, it wasn't the act alone that created anger, but it was the iceberg. Sometimes, it's what leads up to a drama, and what occurs after, that creates function or dysfunction. Using awareness, we can put sovereignty and integrity in our life raft and when we sense a shark is circling, we can whack it with a paddle before it jumps out and bites us. The shark is any emotion, person, place or thing that knocks you off-balance. Those who have been abused know that one word can set us off, on a downward spiral. Determined to comprehend the meaning of Caroline's words even when I felt like I didn't want to paddle any further, I choose to no longer play the victim. What I didn't know was just how close her words matched my life and how they would eventually help me achieve forgiveness. The words were seeds planted in my internal Garden of Eden.

Some years later, another friend enlightened me to *The Little Soul and the Sun* by Neale Donald Walsch. Hear it more than once in a different form from a different source? Another seed? I'm going to sound bite here so you may want to read these books for their full value. Both, explain about the agreements we make before we enter this world and the subsequent forgetting that occurs. Both talk about those who love us so much that they have willingly lowered their vibration so that we can experience who we truly are. Must be song time; "Brass in Pocket" by the *Pretenders*. You know, Chrissie sings about being *special,* and so is the *Little Soul*. Hmm…and maybe "Creep" by *Radiohead*. That's interesting. That means we have two songs titled "Creep" in this book and two creeps in my story. I swear that is just synchronicity. Anyway, being special, the Little Soul chooses as his lesson and story to BE "forgiving." This can't occur one sided; there has to be the other side of the story, someone and something to forgive. They both have to forget before they incarnate, so the drama of the story can play out. Those books already make the point, so why bother with this one? Just kidding!

Many years after working on me, healing myself, and processing the idea of forgiveness, something would still resurface and bother me on a low level. I remember being in workshops, and when someone brought up sexual abuse, it didn't have much of a charge on me anymore. The anger and disgust were gone towards my experience, but not towards the topic. Still there was this nagging, low level anxiety and I would beat myself up about having it. I began to journal as a tool to understand my emotions. I could puke, vent, hiss, and spit on paper, and no one needed to see it or hear it but me, and I was getting it out of my body so it wouldn't eat me up and make me sick. No one was being victimized as long as I kept the words to myself, not even me. Sometimes I would ceremonially tear it up and burn it as an attempt to let go.

Numerous times I considered contacting the anti-hero in my story. From experience, my direct confrontation of people while trying not to be confrontational and be in my heart was not always received so well. It takes people off guard, especially when it's an issue people want to avoid. Even when it's not big, it can be difficult for others if they have not learned about self, and ego. Sexual abuse is more than an issue; it's a huge problem. Writing gives others a chance to figure out how they feel before they respond. Remember, they may choose not to respond at all. This is a place where you have to ask yourself if you can be at peace either way.

Once my emotions were under control, and my authentic self was in charge, I was able to express from a place of heart-centered feeling, and I wrote to my antihero asking for an apology.

My antihero did respond, and more bravely than some of the people who were supposed to love and support me. My antihero mustered the strength and courage to face our battle and offered peace in the form of a *sincere* apology with no "but" attached. There were no excuses; no blame, only accountability. His shaking voice in the offering, evidenced bravery and authenticity. I could hear the regret. Then came the words, **"I don't even know who I was back then...I know what I did was wrong, but I don't even know that guy."** OH, MY Gandhi! He was asleep! Waking up!—that's what I was being taught all along. We all have to wake up—the stories by Neale and Caroline, Keith's workshops. Geez, I'm slow. Nah! I just needed time to heal and the courage to go to the origination point of my pain, so I could integrate that truth in between and let go. It wasn't all about me, but it was my awareness and persistence in seeking an answer that created a resolution in such a profound way. The elements were there; **appreciation** for an apology with no denial that it was easy to **accept**, a moment of pure **joy** came though the **fulfillment** of a desire to let go, the **freedom** to **forgive** and **peace** at last ran from the bottom of my feet to the top of my head with unconditional **love** at the center.

How can you hate someone who has been the catalyst for so many other lies to be exposed, no matter what kind of lie it is? We must learn to forgive and have sympathy for the devil and the devil inside.

Wow! That deserves a big deep breath. That's a feeling to hold onto. That deserves a moment of silence in the divine connectedness of oneness. That's a new origination point to tap into when you need an energy boost. **Forgiveness**; free at last, free at last! (Reference -

Martin Luther King, Jr.). With freedom and forgiveness comes "Amazing Grace" – *John Newton*. Give a listen to any version – I cannot ever listen to this song without tears.

I don't know what it took for my antihero to wake up or how awake he is now. I only know that I forgave him. Now, I only hope that he forgives himself.

Achieving forgiveness for abuse of any kind is not simple. You can't just wish it away or send it away with love. I would never discount someone's feelings whose abuse, pain, anger and suffering run much deeper.

If for whatever reason you don't want direct contact, but you want peace, try the process of going to the person's higher self. Maybe you already know what you want to say to them or maybe you already know what you want to hear, or maybe those words will show up during the process. Ask for what you want. Get as clear as possible with the intent that this is to heal you. For this experience to be fulfilling, you cannot be harboring the fugitives of resentment or anger. If they show up, allow and embrace the feelings until they let go. They may not be gone, but you will feel a certain sense of release. Processing any of the energies may take several—reverse that—it may take many attempts and may take years. Persevere. Embrace the spectrum of possibilities as you learn to embrace yourself. There is time along the journey. Make it, take it and let the journey unfold naturally. It's never too late. Remember, the not okays only exist in 3rd dimension.

"I'm late. I'm late for a very important date." – *White Rabbit, Alice in Wonderland.*

If you are an abuser looking for forgiveness, and you cannot contact the person or persons you hurt, then go to their higher self and ask. Be sincere and be in integrity. Follow the same process.

The idea of embracing the whole spectrum of myself was given to me by a very powerful ancestor in a channeled reading, *Anna*. She was *Yeshua's* grandmother. She said, "There are many Marthas; you must learn to embrace the full spectrum of Martha." I get it now. Embracing my anger led to acceptance. In the past, even the word "embrace" was a problem. Why would I want to embrace anything that caused so much pain? I get it now. I AM GOOD. Evil has collided with Live. Integration has occurred. I've stepped to the other side.

Another time, Anna came to me in my sleep. As I awoke, she said, "Go back to sleep. We are incorporating the Christ consciousness in you." I could not lift my head from the pillow or move my body, and I was clearly awake. I asked for help. Here it was. Anna provided me with messages before I contacted the anti-hero. Asking was something that I had to learn after I learned to feel worthy. While I was getting some help, but not everything that I needed to support me from the outer world, help came in a form that I never expected. I don't even have words to describe the depth of my gratitude. Helpers are all around us. We simply have to be open to pure source, and things will manifest in the KNOW TIME.

But there is still more: the other side. I hold the faith that someday, everyone will awaken and all aspects of our environment will no longer be toxic. There is always hope. Maybe someday evil will be forgotten.

Being told to simply forgive, simply let go, or just send love while containing elements of truth, for me, was simply chaos out of order. Discord caused me to take necessary steps in my journey out of order. The disorder caused me to take miss steps (make mistakes). Sometimes I got tripped up which caused me to fall on my face, which made me feel like I wanted to fall on my sword. But, my sword was the sword of truth which enabled me to cut through the discord. Once I figured out the solution to the equation, order came out of the chaos. Cutting the cords that were cutting into my skin allowed the wounds to heal. Even though there may be battle scars, they do not prevent me from taming the dragons. It may be this way for you, too. Persevere. Find order to your chaos. Know yourself.

In my awareness, it has crossed my MIND and my heart that I allowed myself through conditioning to believe that being responsible and independent meant not asking for help. Being independent can simply mean you are stable with or without assistance. Go to your heart center and ask what it knows using all your chakras as a high counsel or a round table. And it's okay to ask for perspective outside of that table. Remember that it isn't necessary to carry heavy armor all the time.

Your story has endless possibilities. Choose a way that ultimately brings you peace. Find the right first steps for you. It's okay to back up, observe, and have a do-over. It is the only way you will ever be free from the evil beast. It's not the players or you who are the evil; it's whatever energy is holding you back from living fulfilled.

You see, for me, it wasn't that I hadn't let go, as I was accused. It was about bringing a karmic cycle to a conclusion. Merlin would call them the "old ways." Here is an illustration. Near the conclusion of the movie *Merlin,* with Sam Neill and Miranda Richardson, Merlin says:

"You can't fight us or frighten us. You're just...not important enough anymore. We forget you Queen Mab."

After Merlin says this, the evil Queen Mab tries to deceive Merlin one last time by offering a statement of false love for him, but Merlin isn't buying it. Everyone has a capacity for love, even the evil queen, but her love obviously came with conditions. The movie is definitely worth a watch as so many more metaphors are presented.

Forgetting only comes when it isn't important enough to remember anymore. I can't forget because there are too many who are suffering, and they need help to find their path to end suffering.

Many need help so they can take the evil within and turn it around to live, and allow the two points to collide and merge into divinity.

This is the "why bother"! This is the Holy Grail. This is your divine connection to God.

Chapter 17

Letting Go

Now might be a good time to reread the first paragraph in Chapter 3. It's really difficult to "just let go" or "just send love" when something deeper is holding us back from being able to "just let go," without pushing whatever it is into denial. For me, when I don't immediately let go, it's because some part of me deeply believes that things *can* be different, and that it just may take time and perseverance for that difference to show up. Discovering the "aha" to what it will take to let go is like a treasure hunt. Lots of searching and tools are involved but when you find the gold, it is quite rewarding. Because some issues are bigger and deeper than others, it can really piss you off when someone says *just* let go or assumes that because you are still searching that you haven't made progress towards letting go. It's especially annoying when said by someone who has not faced their own drama, and they are telling you that "you **have to** let go" with that disapproving head-bobble. In this case, please "send them a little love," no matter how hard it might be.

Some would rather say, "why bother" out of fear of rejection and disappointment than to face an issue head on. That's not truly letting go. Granted, there are times when being at a level of acceptance is good enough. There can be elements of both letting go and acceptance within the same issue where we can still be at peace.

Interestingly the place where denial is buried could be the same place where treasure is discovered; the convergence point. When you keep digging because your search isn't complete, the first thing you will want to let go of is whether or not someone approves of the digging because it makes them uncomfortable.

We hear talk about regret. Regret about things said, not said, done or not done, before a loved one passed away or regret something wasn't said sooner. Again, it is only fear that holds us back from opening up our hearts. You see; I actually listen and in listening to others talk about regret, I decided I didn't want regret in my life no matter how many times others judged I might be doing something that I would regret. My perseverance has often been perceived by naysayers, finger-pointers and deniers as me not letting go when I knew I was making progress along the path of discovery. Some equations are *simply* more *complicated* than others, and for me, it would be a bigger regret not to seek a solution that was honest and tangible, rather than "just" letting go from a false place of denial. Treasure is usually buried and not found randomly laying on the surface.

When we judge someone or someone judges us by saying, "they will never change" or "can't change" what we are really doing is placing our expectation on the ripeness of a situation.

My ego needed a little validation, so in searching; I found this quote by Eleanor Roosevelt:

"In the long run, we shape our lives, and we shape ourselves. The process never ends until we die. And the choices we make are ultimately our own responsibility."

There are times when we need to step away, take a step back, shift the energy, or give it a rest, that doesn't mean the search is complete. Sometimes we have to obtain clues that will help us discover, from someone who disapproves of our methods during the journey, and their disapproving words can be painful. Particularly, when you are already in pain, it can feel like an ambush. You may not initially perceive these attacks as helpful, as they can, not only knock you off the path but push you over a cliff. Now you need climbing gear to get back up the mountain. While it is more ideal to be supported during a quest, lack of support might be part of the experience. In that case, you not only have to find a map but know that one exists. Then you might have to read the map and follow it but you don't have to share it with everyone. Because, well you know, they might want to take it away from us. If you are on a path of discovery, this may be your experience.

Let me offer a little more honesty about something I was not proud of, but determined to change. Hate and anger consumed a big part of my heart. I didn't want to admit this to anyone. I knew, if I was going to have one regret in my life, it would be not letting go of these two feelings completely. Particularly, since so much of it was directed towards my mother. My honesty about this sets off a lot of judgment in others, and you can feel belief and egos rise at the mere mention of the word "mother."

We often, hear talk about love-hate relationships. Well, mine was really off balance because of all the unconscious things she said, didn't say or do. I searched and searched for years to find one happy memory; something that I could appreciate. To this day, I can find only one, but there is one, and I cling to it. It was the day, I took her to the Grand Canyon and I saw an emotional expression of awe and wonder. It was an energy that I had never experienced emanate from her. Her day to day routine was moving from one chore to another, and there was rarely eye contact without a look of wounded ego or scorn. She seemed to thrive on sadness, the tragedy of illness or death, but trivialized emotional pain. It gave me joy to see that she was capable of experiencing a moment of honest joy and not pretend happiness.

We all need to make clear conscious choices as to the importance of clearing things up or just letting go. Discern and "choose your battles wisely." If you choose to have a direct clearing of the air with someone, recognize that they may view it as confrontational. With egos at play, this is bound to happen. You can ask yours to sit on the bench, but it might jump in and cause a penalty if it feels you need protection, particularly when you are facing an opposing ego. Prepare for battle but don't make it a battle even if it starts to feel that way, otherwise you will end up with battle fatigue and possibly trigger a PTSD response. Remember that what you say might not be what someone else hears, and what you hear might not be what they are trying to say. It's best to be unattached to any particular outcome in case your good intention and early attempts at clearing the air backfires. Accept; that sometimes, our good intentions cause us to be perceived as "the bad guy." Remember that peace negotiations often require more than one meeting. Stay in your heart, hold to your good intention, and stay out of limiting beliefs and expectation. Your odds are fairly good that you will be pleasantly surprised by your feelings towards the outcome even if that outcome is a complete disengagement and letting go.

Allow yourself and others room for growth. Just because you had a particular outcome in one circumstance doesn't mean you will get exactly the same outcome in another (unless there is a glitch in the matrix). If you get similar reactions in multiple attempts, it's time to not only look in the mirror, but also step through the looking glass. Doing the same thing over and over and expecting a different response; that's insanity, right? Maybe you have an other-worldly agreement to break a dysfunctional cycle and end the insanity, so take a different approach or walk away. Exercise your free will and choose wisely. It is always a good idea to ask the divine, *what would it take to ultimately bring peace and letting go?* Notice how the order of the words, peace and letting go, feels internally.

This all sounds like basic knowledge. Right? But, how often do we end up allowing ourselves to participate in unnecessary drama? On the other hand, how are we ever to reach peace and letting go, unless we engage in the turmoil that helps us discover and create what we want? This means, in the stages of clearing a big issue; you could have controversy that isn't comfortable or pretty, but how can you ever repair a relationship that is worth repairing without addressing issues with sincerity? You may find that through the process, other relationships will improve before the one that really bugs you improves.

Do you think I didn't have guilt when people would say, "but she's your mother," "you have to love her," or "at least you have a mother?" Of course I did, and I could see their point, but all I could feel was that I didn't have a mother; I had a caretaker. I am not saying that my feelings were right, I am saying that is how I felt. This was a battle worth taking the time and effort to learn how to get over and let go of, even though she still doesn't understand how badly sexual abuse affected me. She would say things like "We all have problems" or "When are you going to stop this" or "Well, I don't know what you expect me to do." I just wanted a small taste of kindness and compassion specific to the sexual abuse issue.

With my ego still at play being triggered by words that did not express support and getting pissed-off, I had to stay on the path to discover what it would take to help me let go. With a really deep issue, you can go to counseling the rest of your life, or you can just get energy work but without using multiple methods and taking breaks from the drama, it's not likely you will get very far.

Sometimes we are so wrapped up in the search that when something is set before us that we dismiss it. Shame on me since one of my piss-me-offs, was having my feelings dismissed. I watched a documentary about abuse by a Catholic priest, and the parents of the victims were devastated. They expressed love and support to their children, when I hadn't even heard my mother say, "What happened to you was wrong." Then again, who knows what kind of awareness I would have achieved if I hadn't experienced it in this way. I may not have been so driven. The memory of my mother saying she "wished I had been a good Catholic girl" made me think, "yeah, okay, a good Catholic that covers up and protects pedophilia, but doesn't accept gays, divorce or birth control." Yeah, okay, that's what I wanna be hypocritical and prejudice." No disrespect intended for Catholics, but my experience triggers repulsion for the rampant abuse of power.

171

I kept asking the universe for answers, and I would still have people tell me I wasn't asking for help, or I wasn't asking the right questions or the right entity, and would wonder how they could know that I wasn't doing it right. I was asking alright. Some things just take longer to sink in, and are judged by people who say they understand, but don't.

While I recognized divine intervention, initially I took this experience quite lightly. There was this strange message on my voicemail confirming a Deeksha class. So I called back and said, "I didn't sign up for any class, but I am intrigued, and did whoever signed me up, pay for it too? " We eventually solved the mystery and while I questioned time and money, the way it unfolded told me this was important.

During the class, we did an exercise with two circles of participants. The outside circle would whisper into the ear of the inside circle something they wished their parents had said. Maybe I was only hearing what I wanted to hear, but I was hearing an awful lot, of "I love you" and "I'm sorry." Silly me, it took a couple of years to realize that not only is that what I wanted to hear directly from my mother, but that I would have to ask for it, that my mother probably never heard it so she didn't give any importance to saying it. Not because it wasn't important to me, but she never placed enough value on herself to ask for what she wanted. What did I have to lose? I already accepted my feelings being dismissed, rejection and disappointment. I wasn't attached to the outcome and I didn't care what others believed. If I didn't get what I wanted, at least by asking, I would know whether or not this was something I should continue to pursue.

When we choose to deal with something that is uncomfortable, always check in with the heart. See if it feels in alignment with the rest of the body. Let go of the doubt or overconfidence coming from the ego. Thank the ego for showing up, offering reminders and being a good teacher. Tell the ego to take a backseat, or if it wants, it can sit in the front row but only as a spectator. It has already played enough starring roles in the past, and it's time to retire and enjoy the show. If

172

the ego jumps in let the authentic self be the director, call "cut," take a deep breath, center, focus, and speak from your heart. When you check into your feelings from a perspective of heart-centered consciousness, and you can clearly see aspects where your ego is at work, you can honor and embrace that part and make choices that are clear, conscious and concise. That doesn't mean you won't stumble, so be brave. When you do this, even if the other person is unconscious, unaware, still operates primarily from the ego, it is difficult for them to dispute truth.

"It is unwise to be too sure of one's own wisdom. It is healthy to be reminded that the strongest might weaken, and the wisest might err." — *Mahatma Gandhi*

Often we feel like we "shouldn't have to ask" and I heard my mother say that time and time again. There is truth to that, but if we have something we deeply want to let go of, and if we are sure of what it is that we want, then no one is stopping us. I was so moved by the emotions, care and compassion that other families offered to victims, that I either had to have this for myself, or I had to accept that I would never get that, remembering the whole time that the depths of an individual's emotions vary. I was willing to accept the smallest morsel.

When I called, the first thing, I asked was if we could have an honest heart to heart conversation without ego. Every time I heard ego, in myself, I would stop, acknowledge it to her and start over. When I heard ego and sarcasm in her, I would stop and point it out and ask her to "start over." My battle plan was laid out strategically until I was ready to go in for the kill and tell her what I wanted. I needed to open the space for her to be authentic, otherwise any words that I wanted to hear would have just been pacifying. When I felt the crack open, I spoke up and said: "You know mom, friends and strangers have been able to say "What happened to you was wrong,

173

I'm sorry that you had to go through that, and I never heard you say those words."

Her ego started to come up, and she said "Well."

That's all she said: "Well." Obviously, I had to be the one to perpetuate this conversation.

So I asked: "What does that mean, mom? Well?"

She said: "Well, I thought I did." She also admitted she doesn't know how to express very well.

I said: "No, you didn't and I would like to hear it."

There was silence and I said, "really, I want to hear you say it." "Say what?" "I want to hear you say that what happened to me was wrong."

She started to say, "Well, I'm sorry but..." I had to cut her off. I said, "If you follow I'm sorry with a "but" it's not sincere." She stopped and said her version of what I wanted to hear. "I asked, do you really mean that?" She said; "Yes" and I could hear the sincerity.

In the past, I forgave her for so many things, knowing that she only did the best that she could. Hearing those words was all I needed out of our relationship and all I needed to let go.

The naysayers didn't give her enough credit to be able to handle what I had to say, nor did they give me enough credit to say it from a heart centered place that would allow her to speak authentically. Letting go isn't about just burying, forgetting or playing nice. It can be turned into much more. "Hallelujah!" – *Leonard Cohen*. Find a version of the song that suits you and listen.

I still see her as being emotionally stuck at a young age, but maybe somewhere in the cosmos this was our agreement, providing me a way to fully comprehend something that I can share with the world. I no longer see her as pathetic, only as a soul whose light was never allowed to shine and in the reciprocal; I can allow myself to feel love.

Why did I listen to others for so long? What's the worst that could have happened? She would get pissed, act hurt? I'd be disappointed? I was already disappointed. Not confronting her left an unknown. Even if she hadn't stepped up, I would recognize the inability, apologized for pushing her too hard, and I could let go. The naysayers were expecting to me to feel something I couldn't, assuming I wasn't trying, that I was being stubborn, and I was the one making mistakes that would create regret. I was not. I am not expecting her to change, but my persistence allowed her to open her heart in a way that she might not otherwise have been able to. There was discovery in both of our roles. How can that be wrong?

In return, I offered sincerity by saying, "I have no idea what happened to you, because you have never shared much, but I do know that this dysfunction didn't start with you or me. I suspect; no one ever opened the door that allowed you to open up and speak authentically. So I am saying it, right here, right now, I love you. I have spent a lot of time learning how to tear the walls down around my heart, if you ever want to talk, I am here for you. I am willing to listen." "If there is anything that I can do, I will." Though I do not know for sure that she truly heard my words at least I set out the candle and matches.

I am not saying my mother, and I are best friends, or ever will be. We are too different. So long as she doesn't use the word terrible; I'm good. That's not even true. Because she was capable of giving me what I asked for, I can now just roll my eyes at the word that previously set me into a frenzy. As I said earlier, that's what trauma can do; one word sets you off. Don't discount or belittle your own trauma. There are many people in your life who will say they understand, but they don't.

The length of time something takes to unfold is irrelevant. In the excitement of change, you want others to change too. But, that isn't about you, and you can't expect it to be. Know what energy belongs to you, know what belongs to us and what belongs to them. So often we feel separate and alone forgetting that somewhere in the relationship that there is an "us" and therefore, there is an energy that belongs to the "us." In learning to put shit where shit belongs, some might get tossed back at you, not realizing some of it was yours. This is why when you learn about clearing energy, and you attempt to clear for yourself, unless you also put a little effort into clearing for the other party/parties involved, the energy comes back.

When you are frustrated with your progress and others appear to be succeeding, celebrate and be happy when they have something to celebrate and trust that you will celebrate too. We are all entitled to feel joy. Don't allow any to be taken from you. If you feel jealousy, sit in your spectator seat and see what aspects of the scenario you can appreciate. Let go of "why me or why not me?" Jealousy comes from perceived lack. Instead tap into your unique idea of fulfillment so you can let go of jealousy and allow your unique idea of joy to show up. Song time; all this jealous talk reminds me of *Black Crowes'* "Jealous Again."

To let go you may want to follow the idea of detachment from what has happened, what is to happen, and what may or may not happen. Detaching contains elements to help you begin to feel what letting go really is. It is surrendering to the divine but not to defeat. Align with spirit. Maintain integrity. Ask yourself: *Am I coming from a place of deeply rooted belief that may or may not be true? Have I surrendered to the realm of possibility? What will it take for me to let go now? What is it that my soul wants me to know?* (*Queens of the Stone Age,* "No One Knows")

Don't forget to breathe, particularly in and out of the heart. Do that now. It's supernatural.

God is energy. God is love. God is peace. Say to yourself; *I am good. I am god. I am energy. I am peace. I am love.*

Once you have reached a level of acceptance, forgiveness seems to follow automatically. Now, you can begin to feel the letting go process become tangible in your mind, body, soul, and external environment. Offer appreciation and gratitude.

If you want to, you can check your integration, go back in, and just notice if there are any old feelings still there. Do not be afraid if anything remains. Hold on to what you have gained, but don't grip so tightly that you create a new belief. Let go of the self-imposed hell you have been in and celebrate the progress. Amazing!

After some rest, you can let go of more. Ask; *What else does my soul wanted me to experience?* Let's consider that the feeling you want to let go of is the inability to trust because you experienced the feeling of betrayal. Ask yourself: *What would it feel like right now if I were able to see this as just an experience—an experience that I will be stronger for once I get through it? Can I trust that I chose this experience so that I could unlock another door to the authentic me? What does it feel like to let go and surrender to the universe in full and complete trust? What does it feel like to trust myself? Allow the feelings to enter your energetic field.*

Breathe through each question. Feel the question in your heart and let it settle in any other part of your body that it wants to. Breathe and say: "Everything has an equal and opposite reaction. From this experience of trust being utterly broken and shattered, I will at some point be presented with an opportunity to fully embrace trust as I increase my awareness. I trust the universe, trust myself, and trust that there is a much bigger picture. (*Tool—"Schism"*) I trust that all the pieces will fall into place at the right time when the time is ripe, in the know time. I trust my heart, trust my gut, and trust unconditional love and support. I accept support and know that I am supported by unseen forces." Feel that love and support by breathing love in and out, bringing in love on the in-breath and sending out old ugly crap on the out-breath or down into the core of the earth, where the old energy can be transmuted and returned to you in equal but opposite feeling. It will return not as a force to be reckoned with but as a divine blessing and gift of sight, sense, sound, feeling, and knowing, with an attractive fragrance and an explosion of tasting the good life through letting go.

Don't overthink it. Let the feeling wash over you, cleanse you. Letting go might begin with letting in. Try it both ways. Breathe it both ways.

Try it. Don't just read and intellectualize it. Honor that you are a spiritual being, having human experience. Honor that you are here to master life. You are not here to cling to the illusion of the matrix. Give yourself the opportunity to become a master.

Let go of not being worthy of being a master. **Let go of not being a worthy of being a master.** Let go of not being worthy of being a master.

Chapter 18

A Few Notes on Meditation and Manifestation

I planned on doing an expanded chapter on meditation, but we are going to wrap it up and save it for another time when we can expand on *know time,* which you have heard me talk about here the *whole time*. Of course, that will have to include past lives, which is past time, but if time is happening simultaneously, then do past lives really exist? Hmm. Thanks, Einstein, for your theories on time; they are divine. No, I never read the whole theory on time. On time—actually, "about time" would have been more appropriate—I've just pulled sound bites. After all, we create our own reality, or should that be "manifest our own reality," or both.

Next time, I will dive into detail regarding my version of the spiral meditation, which was given to me by a divine ancestor in a channeled reading. In the meantime, there's that time thing coming up again, and my guides are telling me that this book is out of time, except for this last piece on meditation.

At this point, in the evolution of humanity, it is essential to learn how to **expand** our consciousness. To move beyond, we first "have to" *feel* on tangible level and we "have to" **breathe.**

Once we learn how to expand, we must then learn to collapse it back into our being. This is how we learn to feel on a tangible level. In practicing the expansion and contraction, the sending and receiving of energy is how what we create manifests. First, we create the energy, then we implement by sending it out, and we manifest by bringing it back in.

Breathing in and out, sense love, send it out, and bring it back into our being. Observe the feeling. What does that feel like?

Do this with your attention while you are breathing: send it out then bring it back in. Observe it. What does it feel like?

If you can't feel it in your heart, go to another place calling for your awareness and start there; flip-flop your attention between this place and your heart.

You get what you give. We've used all these metaphors, we've been beating around the bush, dropping all these hints, but consider doing this simply with energy and start to observe what happens around you. When you observe, you will begin to know what your soul wants to embrace. There is a direct correlation between creation and manifestation with the sending and receiving through the breath; expand and collapse. This is one of the ways the universe works, and as part of the universe, so do you. But do not dismiss that there is something beyond. What's beyond is part of what we do with the spiral while it still includes expanding and collapsing; it happens in an expanded way.

We've heard about putting your intentions out there and then allowing or waiting to see what shows up, but we haven't necessarily focused our attention on the consistency of sending and receiving. We've been told to sit still and be quiet. While reaching still point has exponential value, it isn't where most of us can start. We also have not necessarily been told that creation/manifestation is the actual purpose of bringing the breath in and then sending it out. We've been told to let go on the out breath and bring a cleansing breath in, but we haven't really been taught from a larger, more expanded viewpoint, or to do it in the opposite direction. Perhaps spend a little time paying attention to what occurs in between. Perhaps spend a little time repeating the word peace as you breathe in and out through the heart.

In our impatience, we want to get to the beginning and the end too quickly. We want the breath to be both local and global. Practice both to aid in healing and expanding into the global consciousness.

Some are sitting around ah'ing and om'ing but not really grasping what it is that they are doing or why, so they say, "Why bother?" Sometimes, besides coming from the heart, we need an intellectual aha to keep us going. Honestly, I am not knocking anyone who is implementing any type of meditative practice. I ah and Om, too, on a regular basis! It has value and adds to the betterment of our world, but, with a greater comprehension, the intent will be more purposeful and directed. Many are still focused on the thoughts in their heads, and this prevents them from meditating because of overthinking and judging the process. It simply takes a bit more comprehension and commitment, and breath is the best place to start. When the intent is more clearly directed, the energy will be more powerful; thereby, impressing upon you, me, or us that we *are* all divinely connected. In this knowing, everything begins to vibrate at a higher, more positive level. In this case, higher and positive are appropriate. We only play in the lower vibrations to create a clear concise comprehension of our intent.

There are times when you will want to direct attention to something specific that needs healing. Other times you will want to take your attention of off the thing if it is creating a distraction. Creating a more expanded awareness in your practice of meditation and then collapsing the energy back into yourself can create spontaneous healing. What you heal, could be anything...anything— health, money, relationships, emotional, that's for you to consider.

Focusing too much attention on the specific need in meditation is holding on to the "thing" and not letting it have space to move in or out, because you are clinging too tightly. It's like being desperate. So, yes, set an intention or say a prayer for what it is that you would like to occur. Ask for assistance from a perspective of gratitude and appreciation for any help that will be provided, but do not focus on the "thing" during the meditation. But that doesn't mean you can't give "the thing" a momentary embrace. Let go; then allow whatever wants to show up to show up. You may get an unexpected, pleasant surprise, particularly if it is peace and serenity. If chaos shows up in your day to day life, you will be surprised at how you handle it in a calmer manner and allow it to disappear as quickly.

This is why I love the spiral so much. Not only is the spiral not linear, as time is not linear, but it also represents the expanded and contracted universe. The nonlinear fashion of the spiral breaks down the stereotype of doing anything in a certain way which allows the chakras to support one another more effectively, opening pathways you didn't think possible.

That doesn't mean you can't follow a straight and narrow path somewhere within that space. You send energy out with the spiral and bring it back into self with the spiral. The spiral spins off energy that is no longer needed or wanted and no longer serves. On the return, clear energy is deposited into the heart, taking all the energy created by the spiral meditation facilitating creation and manifestation. The spiral shows us that the never-ending karmic circle is like the merry-go-round that might be fun for a moment but at some point you want to get off and away from the dizziness from being on too long.

However, do not dismiss beginning with the straight path. Many have told me that they have found the spiral to be too complex in starting the practice of meditation and find it simpler to stick with following one path and one color, even if that color is white. Practice breathing into the earth for grounding and bringing the energy up through your body to connect to the divine simultaneously. Focus sending the breath and energy through your body, until you feel the connection. When you are ready, then use the spiral, use the full spectrum, and take your time as you play in between.

When I was given the message about embracing the full spectrum and presented with the spiral, the message was very clear. She said, *"I don't want you to do the spiral meditation; I want you to play with it."*

So often in group meditation and it seems that without fail, someone will say, "I didn't feel like I went anywhere." Resist judging yourself and the process. When this happens, use it as a subtle reminder to focus on the pattern of the breath, allowing it to go in and out of the heart as you move it through various parts of your body. If you can't silence the idle chatter in your brain, repeat the word peace to yourself or choose another word that suits you. Some meditations are simply more profound than others. If you let go of the judgment, you may find that through the meditation, messages and synchronicities will show up later.

If you are worrying, you are not in present moment. Placing judgment and expectation on your meditation takes you out of present moment where, with practice, you can achieve still point, but you don't need to achieve it each and every time. Instead, honor yourself for giving yourself the time in the present moment, and the universe will honor you back. You can even say this to yourself: *I am honoring myself by giving myself this moment of pure peace.* You may notice that you feel the peace in your heart, but you may also notice that it goes up and out through the top of your head and washes over you, creating peace for your inner and outer world. It's all about practice. And when you begin to judge practice, think about the fact that the doctor you respect so much still calls what he/she does a practice.

Often the people who utilize the best healing practices will say, "It's not me; it's an energy that works through me." With that said, much of what I have said in this book came through me from many other sources. Some of the sources were ones I was very aware of and others that I was unaware of, but nonetheless, I Am, infinitely grateful and awe full.

My friend once called attention to my unawareness that I was channeling Roald Dahl. My response was, "Who's that?"

The answer: "You know, he wrote Willy Wonka."

So, in his honor, even though he didn't write the song but obviously was an inspiration for the writing of it, please take the time to read the words of "Pure Imagination" by *Leslie Bricusse* and *Anthony Newly* from the 1971 movie *Willy Wonka and the Chocolate Factory*, and listen to whatever version you choose. If you are going to think of anything during meditation, use pure imagination.

Conclusion

There is no need for blame. Accountability, yes, but blame not so much. Blame keeps us stuck in the past. We are all a product of societal conditioning, good or bad. Karma is ours to break. We can all start to say, "Thank you," to those who played starring roles in our stories and give credit where credit is due.

Have you ever noticed how when you go to the movies, most people start to leave as soon as the last scene of the story ends? In order to gain complete mastery of our lives, it could be beneficial to review the credits at the beginning and the end of any particular storyline.

They say the teacher will show up when the student is ready. Or is it the students will show up when the teacher is ready, or the teachers will show up when the student is ready? The teachers show up in many forms and many ways to play starring, supporting and non-supporting roles to varying degrees for a season, a reason, or a lifetime of everyone's story.

Even the words, "I will teach you," have two different contexts when said with kindness and compassion or with anger and revenge.

The karmic cycle is exactly what is keeping this world in such a mess—full of wars, hate, and controversy from full blown war down to arguments among family and neighbors that we so loudly proclaim to want to end. So, in this cycle, we must learn not only to attempt to let go of the bad, but you may have to be brave enough to step up and also let go of some of the good. This is where the power of the positive fails and where negative gets a bad rap. Sometimes negatives can be a good thing if you are letting go of a little positive to fully and completely heal the negative. If you are brave enough to do that, you may just find that you step into an expanded world that is full of joy, fulfillment, freedom, and peace, where acceptance, appreciation and unconditional love are at home in self. Focus on what you can, not on what you can't, but don't use *can't* as an excuse.

Sometimes the mirror technique has great value for us to see what is being reflected back, but often I would find it annoying. No matter how annoyed, I knew there was still something I was missing. It would benefit all of us to look not only at our own reflection, but the background, foreground and all around.

One of the reasons people judge you is because misery loves company. They want you to be stuck where they are. They fear not having a partner to be in misery with. Many are fearful of letting go of the smallest amount of happiness that they are willing to sacrifice themselves to hang on to that which is familiar, no matter how limiting or emotionally unhealthy. If you don't want this to be you, don't let it be you. Place a little focus on the background. See how differently things appear. It's not about you or me; it's about all of us. We must remember that it is not just difficult for us to let go of others but for them to let go of us. If we could all learn to loosen our grip on the illusory reality that has been miscreated, we could all experience more freedom.

In creating change, our internal knowing presents us with the clarity of knowing that if we stop connecting the circle and transform it into a spiral with a full spectrum of color, observe the expansion and contraction, and allow some of that energy to spin off and other energy to jump on, a whole new world is created. We have created a whole new ways of seeing, feeling, perceiving, and interpreting. Recognition comes in seeing how our lives equate exactly to the spiral universe that we are playing in: the good and the bad, the yin and the yang, and the new that we are capable of creating. Being stuck in a karmic cycle does not serve a divine purpose.

For those of you who smugly sit back and latch onto the expression that "karma is a bitch," remember that circle comes back around, so you might just get bit in the ass when you least expect it.

Karma is the reason we wonder why bad things happen to good people. So why continue to play with it at all? Eye for an eye simply doesn't work. The harsh reality is that if you choose to stay stuck in karma, then you are part of the problem, not part of the solution.

This goes back to what Keith Varnum said in the very first workshop I attended on heart-centered consciousness: "The hardest thing you will ever do is let go of people in your life." Talk about coming around full circle, I mean full spiral. Little did I realize that this meant letting go of a little good to eliminate a lot of the bad.

"The best teachers are those who tell you where to look but don't tell you what to see."—*Alexandra K. Trenfor*

Sometimes we sabotage ourselves when we walk away from something good, because we didn't see the good. For me, there was a deep knowing that what I was leaving behind would return in another form. What I was leaving came with too much control and toxin than I could bear. My internal knowing said, *"Leave or die."* At the time, there were lots of excuses that I no longer need. The truth will do; like it or not. The details don't matter; listening to my knowing did.

Letting go of a little good and learning to come from a more expanded perspective, releases internal suffering and allows joy into present-moment awareness in a fresh, new, expanded way which can be appreciated on a much deeper level. Conversely, sometimes holding onto a little good, drives us toward the light.

Thank you to all the actors who lowered their vibration so much that they forgot who they truly are; it allowed me to awaken to the divine spiral of life. I was burned to the core, and the eruption at the center transformed me into who I am meant to be. ("Eruption" – *Van Halen*) Thank you for being such good participants. I hope that once and for all, we will break the karmic cycle and only play in the light. And thank you for joyous eruptions shared with those who offered me love and support.

Come with me to a world of pure imagination. We can let go of hatred, bitterness, anger, and resentment. We can change those feelings to strength, sincerity, clarity, and divine purpose.

So, while earlier I cautioned you in using sound bites, now I will state a contradiction. Take some of the sound bites from your teachers and run with them, play with them, and expand on them. When you do, you begin to notice the synchronicity of every interaction in your life becoming more joyful and friendlier. You won't attract as many of the Negative Nellies, the Downer Dollies, the Judgmental Jims, and Apathetic Adams. You will simply not attract as much of the things that are perceived as unpleasant. You may even begin to notice that less begins to feel like more. You will smile more, and instead of dragging your feet, you may begin to feel each movement as more of a dance. *Ung Salome Gaia*—this is a message given to me during a walking meditation in the desert. My translation: Dance to the rhythm of Mother Earth. When you do this, everything around you that was maniacal will become magical. Things will light up, will liven up, and will become illuminated; things will flow and dance.

The magic may at first appear random. Maybe it is, maybe it isn't. But, each and every time you change your perception, it creates more order to the chaos. I've seen it; I've lived it even with the devil inside. Wait, "devil" is "lived" backwards. There it is again. One last song: *INXS's* "The Devil Inside." Is it art imitates life or life imitates art? Or both? Regardless, things change when you open your heart, your will, your discernment, your creativity, your voice of truth, your inner stability, and your ability to take what you see with both eyes and create one unified vision, bringing that around full spiral to your crowning glory of wisdom. That's the real spiral; that's the real chakra system. To be continued in book two.

And now that this book has finally come to a conclusion, let me remind you what good teachers our children can be in the spiral of life. I was questioning the premise of a TV show that my teen was describing, and her response was, "Really, Mom, does everything have to have purpose?"

To which I responded, "No, you are right. So what should we do that is completely pointless?"

Okay, I lied. There is another one more thing. Every culture on our planet has music. It's universal, maybe even galactic. Sound and vibration are healing. Music is creative. Music touches all of our senses. Why do you think we call them Rock Stars or Rock Gods? Duh! I realize that some may be intergalactic beings on a mission or lay over, and many have their own challenges, but who cares? They are really good at teaching us to let go of judgment. So, in honor of a remake, a recreate, a do-over that is better than the original. Wow, talk about judgment and opinion! How about *Adam Lambert* and his rendition of "Mad World"? Thank you, *Roland Orzabal* and *Tears for Fears* for the original. May your tears wash away your fears! Namaste!

Appendix I

Martha's Playlist

To listen to this playlist, go to: www.marthadusage.com and click on the playlist banner.

Acknowledgements: "All Around Me" – *Flyleaf*

Preface: "True Colors" – *Cyndi Lauper*
"Mornin'" – *Al Jarreau*

Introduction: "You Decide" – *Fireflight*
"Magical Mystery Tour" – *Beatles*
"Us and Them" – *Pink Floyd*
"We are Broken" – *Paramore*

Chapter 1: Taking The Journey
"Break the Cycle" – *Staind*
"Man In The Mirror" – *Michael Jackson*

Chapter 2: Contradiction, Perception, Interpretation, Misinterpretation
"Desperate" – *Fireflight*
"If You Love Somebody" – *Sting*
"Wrapped Around Your Finger" – *Police*
"Ring My Bell" – *Anita Ward*
"War" – *performed by Edwin Starr and Bruce Springsteen*
– written by Norman Whitfield and Barrett Strong
"Bomb the World" – *Michael Franti*

Chapter 8: My Mission Statement and Personal Prime Directive
> Sorry, no song. You are free to explore what's in your heart.

Chapter 9: Mastering Third Dimension, Fear and Faith, Integrity

Part A:	"Changes" – *Bowie*
	"What I've Done" – *Linkin Park*
	"Sympathy For The Devil" – *Rolling Stones*
Part B:	"Personal Jesus" – *Depeche Mode or Marilyn Manson*
Part C:	"See Me" – *The Who*
	"All These Things" – *The Killers*
	"Man In A Box" – *Alice In Chains*
	"Down With The Sickness" – *Disturbed*
	"She Talks To Angels" – *Black Crowes*

Chapter 10: Know Thyself

Part A:	"Getting To Know You" – *Rogers and Hammerstein*
	"One Way" – *Blonde*
Part B:	"Big Shot" –*Billy Joel*
	"Fashion" – *Bowie*
	"Teach Your Children" – *Crosby, Stills, Nash, Young*
Part C:	"Creep" – *Stone Temple Pilots*

Chapter 11: Personal Responsibility
> "Change The World" – *Eric Clapton*

Chapter 12: It's Not All about You—Two Sides to Every Story
> "Right In Two" – *Tool*
> "I Will Follow" – *U2*

Chapter 13: Acceptance
> "Crawling" – *Linkin Park*
> "Communication Breakdown" –*Led Zepplin*
> "Daughter" – *Pearl Jam*
> "Stand Up" – *Fireflight*

Chapter 14: Dysfunction
"Conjunction Junction"– *School House Rock*
"Save Yourself" – *Stabbing westward*
"Resistance" – *Muse*
"Uprising" – *Muse*
"I'm Free" – *The Who*
"Kashmir" – *Led Zepplin*
"Abracadabra" – *Steve Miller Band*
"No Boundaries" – *Adam Lambert*
"Unbreakable" – *Fireflight*
"Behind Blue Eyes" – *The Who*
"Broken Girl" – *Matthew West*
"Hell is for Children" –*Pat Benatar*
"Voices" – *Alice in Chains*
"Sisters of Avalon" – *Cyndi Lauper*
"Synchronicity I and II" – *Police*
"Respect" – *Aretha Franklin*
"All Right Now" – *Free*

Chapter 15: Unconditional Love and the Heart Pillar Exercise
Sorry, no song. Perfect opportunity to come up with your own.

Chapter 16: Forgiveness and Freedom
"Brass" – *Pretenders*
"Creep" – *Radiohead*
"Amazing Grace" – *John Newton*
"Jealous" – *Black Crowes*
"No One Knows" – *Queens of the Stone Age"*
"Hallelujah" – *Leonard Cohen*
"Schism" – *Tool*

Chapter 17: Letting Go
      "Jealous" – *Black Crowes*
      "No One Knows" – *Queens of the Stone Age"*
      "Hallelujah" – Leonard Cohen
      "Schism" – *Tool*

Chapter 18: A Few Notes on Meditation and Manifestation
      "Pure Imagination" – *Leslie Bricusse*
        and Anthony Newley

Conclusion:
      "Eruption" – *Van Halen*
      "Devil Inside" – *Inxs*
      "Mad World" – *Tears For Fears – Adam Lambert cover*

About the Author

Martha Du'Sage has stepped through the looking glass of dysfunction and sexual abuse to discover, what we can all discover, an end to suffering. Through over 20 years of practicing heart-centered conscious knowing, she has hands-on, rather than clinical experience to share, helping others to see things in a new light regarding their abuse, which creates a peace within.

With one foothold in the conventional world, Martha spent a great deal of time in business, particularly the insurance industry, but she always knew that she had a different purpose. With greater attraction to the unconventional, attempting to break down worn-out paradigms and belief, she found herself more often saying, "who says it has to be that way?" It was that desire to play in the alternative world that led her to seek knowledge from the mystical, creative realms.

Her work is a combination of what she has learned from many teachers of consciousness as well as training in NLP, Deeksha – Oneness Blessing, massage, reflexology, aromatherapy, body wrapping, fitness and nutrition, and more. Besides writing and energy work, Martha creates aromatherapy blends as a compliment to your inner work.

While resisting rigid belief she finds what is considered the unconventional world is actually more natural and authentic. It is the love of nature and the natural that drives her to help others put an end to their struggles. Her studies in consciousness and a desire not to adhere to any one system of belief have led her to practice energy work intuitively. She simply guides whoever she is working with, into their own, state of present moment awareness where she encourages you to embrace the full spectrum of you.

There was a time when Martha found herself in a profession saying, "this is what I do, not who I am." In order to honor the "I AM" presence that is in all of us, she decided it was time to offer her voice to those that have not yet discovered theirs, due to past trauma and abuse. Hence, the birth of this book – *"Why Bother? Because Self-Help is Never Stupid."*

Currently, she is in the process of developing several workshops, including "The Heart Pillar" which was introduced in this book and "Breaking Lack Consciousness." Contact information can be found at www.marthadusage.com. Various private sessions are available to help you discover the "I AM" in you.

About the Cover

This is a last minute addition to the book because interest began brewing around the cover and its meaning.

There are a lot of pissed off people walking around this planet, for many reasons. Some proudly wear that anger, some hide it, some have it under control and then something triggers it (look out) and others are so deep in denial they don't even know it's there. I used to be all of them. Then we have those that are overly emotional and unknowingly actually use this as a protection mechanism or avoidance technique. We humans, have different ways of coping with emotion. Our less than ideal emotion often comes from of some form of abuse and often we feel victimized and that even applies to the tough guy or bully. When we feel this way it's just a lack of understanding or lack of seeing the bigger picture in our mastery of third dimension.

Well that was more about the subtitle, but that's where all the symbolism comes in on the cover. The bear represents what happens when the wounded child grows up. There is a raging pissed-off bear inside even if we try to hide it, deny it or ignore it. However, peace is possible when we learn to integrate and operate with the heart as the center rather than the head and ego. That's where the lotus comes in on the bear's heart.

If we don't deal with what lies below the surface, we can explode like a volcano. Hence the volcano in the back-ground and something I use a metaphor in the book a few times. It's helpful to understand it is exactly those volcanic eruptions that we can use to transform like a butterfly and create stability in a chronically unstable world. The balloons can represent lightness but also represent being numb and having your head in the clouds rather than being grounded.

We can be firmly grounded and divinely connected to pure source at the same time. This is how we transform being pissed-off into peace and passion, because the combined elements of being grounded and divinely connected, opens us up to a world of possibility that only existed in the unimagined parts of self.

My wounded child came from being sexually abused by 2 non-blood-related family members. One in 5 girls and one in 6 boys have suffered from some form of abuse and that is only what is reported. My abuse was never report and most that I have met that also suffered abuse or rape never reported it either. This is my way of validating the feeling of being pissed-off, numb, in denial or emotional; to let others know that it's okay if they aren't "over it" yet, but that they can eventually do just that and find peace.

www.ingramcontent.com/pod-product-compliance
Lightning Source LLC
LaVergne TN
LVHW051505080426
835509LV00017B/1925